COFFEE CUP COUNSELING

D0813834

COFFEE
CUP
COUNSELING

HAROLD SALA

NELSON

Thomas Nelson Publishers
Nashville

Published in Nashville, Tennessee, by Thomas Nelson, Inc., and distributed in Canada by Lawson Falle, Ltd., Cambridge, Ontario.

Printed in the United States of America.

Library of Congress Cataloging-in-Publication Data

Sala, Harold J.
   Coffee cup counseling / by Harold J. Sala.
      p.   cm.
   ISBN 0-8407-3036-5
   1. Peer counseling in the church. 2. Bible—Psychology.
I. Title.
BV4409.S24   1989
253.5—dc20   89-12860
                                       CIP

1 2 3 4 5 - 91 90 89

*To my wonderful wife, Darlene,
who has been my closest friend
and best counselor for more
than three decades.*

Contents

Foreword

More advice is given by friends than by all the psychiatrists, psychologists, and counselors put together. And why not? Who is in a better position to give advice than a friend? After all, who knows idiosyncrasies, temperaments, strengths, weaknesses, abilities, and even failures better than a friend? Besides, a person will take advice from a friend when he or she would never consider going to a professional counselor.

This is a book for you who have had little if any training in counseling or therapy, yet find yourselves in the position of helping other people work through personal problems—lay people who work with others as Bible study leaders, Sunday School teachers, fellowship leaders, teachers, deacons, church officers.

This is a book for you who attract people who seem to feel that talking over problems with you will help. I do not intend to make this technical, but easy-to-understand, practical, and scriptural. Most of what Jesus said was communicated in nontechnical language, and He was readily understood.

You have probably never thought of yourself as being someone who could make a significant contribution to the lives of other people, yet when you stop and think of the conversations you've had with friends and acquaintances, you'll recognize that you've dispensed a lot of advice and support.

How to do a better job helping other people work through their problems is what this book is about.

The names of individuals I have described have been changed to protect their identities, but the situations I have written about are a composite of real people who have faced intense, personal problems.

My special thanks to John and Sandi West who provided a quiet place for me to write. I am also grateful to my wife, Darlene, and my daughter Bonnie Craddick, both of whom have offered sound counsel from a woman's perspective. Carol Olson, Norma Collins, Joy Shaw, and Norma Bailey have helped immensely in proofreading the manuscript. And, finally, I want to thank my editor Janet Hoover Thoma for improving the contents of this book by valuable suggestions, thoughtfully and graciously proffered.

Harold J. Sala
Mission Viejo, California

COFFEE CUP COUNSELING

1

You Can Help People!

"What do you think I should do?"

How often have you been asked this question while having a cup of coffee with a friend or in the parking lot as you stood chatting with a friend after a meeting? It may have come at the back fence or in the beauty shop as your friend began to share a rather personal part of her life.

"Well, what do you think I should do?" You're on, friend.

You may not be an Abigail Van Buren.

You may not be a trained counselor.

You may have never even taken a night class in counseling or psychology.

You may never have even thought of yourself as someone who could significantly help anyone else, yet as soon as you say, "Ah, well, here's what I think . . ." you are giving counsel. God has opened a door for you to help someone, perhaps working through you as a channel of divine guidance, using you in a way that you had never considered possible.

It is only natural that we seek the advice and counsel of those who know us and are closest to us. After all, we are comfortable with our peers and can easily relate to them. We are not embarrassed to talk with them about intimate and personal needs, especially when we are relatively sure that they already have some idea of what we are facing. With friends we are not intimidated by the stigma that is often attached to making appointments and going to an office for help.

I am convinced that you do not have to be a psychologist or a clinically trained psychoanalyst to help people. You do not have to be able to interpret dreams or read inkblots or recognize profound psychological insights. Most of the counseling dispensed today is given out by people who have had little training, if any, when it comes to counseling.

Reacting against Freudian psychology and humanistic concepts, which are clearly in violation of God's Word, some Christians have taken a negative position against psychology and counseling in general when they should have taken a negative position against forms of counseling which violate scriptural principles.

The problem is not in giving advice or counsel; it is in giving the wrong kind of counsel. Nonetheless, some have tended to throw out the baby with the bath water.

I have heard people say, "I don't believe in counseling—just preaching and praying!" Yet when a person takes such a position and still says, "I think you should . . ." and suggests a course of action regarding a friend's personal needs, he has put himself in the position of a counselor.

The "anti-counseling" mentality also fails to recognize that the healing ministry of Jesus was the purest psychiatry ever applied to the emotional wounds of hurting men and women.

When I was in college, the founder of the Christian

university I attended reflected a bias of his generation as he said, "Boys [meaning ministerial students], you don't need courses in counseling. All you need is common sense!"

An oversimplification? Yes! Especially since common sense isn't so common anymore!

If we called counseling by some other name—say, discipling or ministering—perhaps it would be more acceptable to some. Paul wrote that we who believe in Jesus Christ have been given "the ministry of reconciliation," which means we bring men and women back into harmony with our heavenly Father and with each other as well (see 2 Cor. 5:18,19).

Helping to heal broken relationships is one of the most significant contributions you can ever make to the lives of other people.

You Have a Mandate to Help People

Writing to the Galatians, Paul instructed, "Brothers, if someone is caught in a sin, you who are spiritual should restore him gently" (Gal. 6:1 NIV). The word Paul used for sin, *paraptoma*, means "false step, transgression, sin."[1] In the context of life today it means a wrong decision, a poor choice, a relationship which is bound to end in disharmony and suffering. It's a strong word. But the action required to help save a person from his fate is gentle but firm, and only those who really care are willing to take the risks of engaging in the process of helping another.

People ask that question, "What do you think I should do?" for a variety of reasons. At times they are simply seeking validation for what they really want to do, and probably will do anyway no matter what you say, but usually that question is asked because a person is uncertain and searching.

"Who am I to tell someone else what to do?" you might be wondering.

Long ago the psalmist wrote, "The godly man is a good counselor because he is just and fair and knows right from wrong" (Ps. 37:30,31 LB).

"Who am I to tell anyone else what to do?"

You are a child of God who has his feet planted on the Rock, Christ Jesus! You don't have to be a Mother Teresa or a Billy Graham. If you have a clear vision to see what your friend cannot see because your judgment isn't clouded by emotional entanglement, you are one through whom God can work.

When I was living in the Philippines and was driving somewhere and had lost my way, I would stop and ask directions. I quickly learned that to say, "I don't know!" may make someone feel he will "lose face." Consequently, when directions were vague and uncertain, I needed to say, "Thank you very much!" and find someone else to ask. But when someone said, "You have to turn around and go back one mile to the first major intersection, and take a hard left turn," I knew that I could follow that person's counsel.

When people ask, "What do you think I should do?" it is often because their judgment has become clouded. Their decision-making process is obscured by issues which make it hard for them to see the consequences of their actions. If your thinking is clear, you become an asset of immeasurable value.

As part of the family of God, we have a responsibility to each other. A family is a series of interlocking relationships, and it is the quality of the relationships that affects the quality of family living. We're like a team of mountain climbers linked together by rope; when one stumbles or falls, another can be an anchor to hold him steady.

Once my son was climbing mountains in Switzerland, and he noticed three climbers on the face of another incline. Suddenly, one lost his footing and fell. The second man was supposed to be his anchor, but that man fell under the weight of the first; then the two of them pulled the third loose. The three tumbled hundreds of feet down the face of that glacier. Fortunately they were able to walk away from the fall.

That's often the way it is when someone makes a bad decision. "It's my life, and I can do with it what I please!" The one who says that seldom sees the consequences of his actions in relationship to the rest of the family members or friends, linked together by the bonds of love forged over the years.

The Bible stresses that we have a responsibility to help brothers and sisters make good decisions. At least fifty-eight times we find "one another" phrases in the New Testament, all expressing some kind of obligation or responsibility we have to each other in the body of Christ. Among the many, you will see we are to:

- Love one another
- Pray for one another
- Bear one another's burdens
- Encourage one another
- Exhort one another
- Admonish one another

In obeying these instructions, you become a counselor.

In many parts of the world, especially around

swampy areas, a condition develops that geologists call "quicksand." An animal or an unsuspecting person who happens to step into this sandy mire is sucked deeper and deeper into the quicksand, and unless that person or animal is rescued, loss of life is certain.

No individual in his right mind would ever intentionally walk into quicksand, right? But once caught in its clutches, the sinking person must have help to get himself out of that situation. So it is with the problems which confront a lot of people. The person who asks, "What should I do?" may feel absolutely overwhelmed. He or she feels the downward pull of a situation which seems hopeless.

That's where you come into the picture. You have every right as well as the responsibility to say, "I think you should . . ."

Avoiding our responsibilities to brothers and sisters simply because we don't consider ourselves to be "professionals" leaves a lot of people hurting who could have so easily been helped.

Helping people through counseling is part of what Paul urged the Galatians to do in bearing each other's burdens and thus fulfilling the great law of love (see Gal. 6:1–5). It is time to begin assuming our responsibility for each other.

Our failure to meet that responsibility has created a vacuum in the Christian community which all too often is filled by unsaved men and women whose counseling techniques violate the principles of God's Word.

If you still are not convinced that you can help people, allow me to point out two very important facts: (1) You have at your disposal the solid direction of the Word of God which is a "lamp to my feet and a light to my path" (Ps. 119:105); and (2) God's Holy Spirit indwells you as His child, and He can give you insight and wisdom far beyond your human capacity (see Rom. 8:9).

You who know Jesus Christ as your personal Lord and Savior have an anchor to reality which lets you throw the lifeline to people being sucked into the quicksand of life by a host of problems.

Let's take a look at the way counseling in this framework of Christian faith enables you to succeed and be effective as a people helper.

Counseling in a Biblical Framework

Recently, I spent a month in the beautiful little country of New Zealand, and during that time I drove an automobile very much like the one I drive at home. Like the car I have, it had four wheels, a horn, and a steering wheel.

Driving was different, however. New Zealanders drive on the left side of the road (no, not necessarily the wrong side). I had to convert my thinking; "Pull to the left instead of the right." I had to keep telling myself, "Watch for cars passing on the right!" It was different, and I never would have arrived at my destination without readjusting my thinking as well as my driving.

Now, when you counsel utilizing the perspective of faith, you've got to convert your thinking as certainly as driving on a different side of the road. Paul told the Corinthians, whose culture and society was very sensual and worldly, if a person is in Christ, he or she was a new person; everything becomes new, he explained (see 2 Cor. 5:17).

Counseling from a biblical perspective doesn't mix the profane and the godly like a man who drives on the left side of the road for a while and then switches over to the other side because he can see the scenery better. The person who counsels in a biblical perspective makes a commitment: He goes God's way no matter what others may think.

Today in some Christian circles there are many people who are weaving back and forth. They are following humanistic principles, advocating and endorsing lifestyles which clearly don't meet with God's approval (because He's given very clear statements regarding the choices of life). In counseling they follow secular models and hold to the teaching of men whose lives are totally out of harmony with Scripture. They sprinkle a few Bible verses here and there throughout their counseling as if to sanctify a pagan system.

God's approach to dealing with our needs is vastly different from the natural man's method of leaving God on the sidelines. Let me get specific in some areas. How does counseling in a biblical framework differ from secular counseling? What are the presuppositions (yes, biases) which you adopt when you are committed to the fact that God is a loving God who knows what is best for His children and has given us direction through the pages of His Word?

Counseling from a Biblical Perspective Recognizes the Authority of God's Word, the Bible

Once an individual recognizes that the Bible is God's "psychiatry," much of the confusion which surrounds our lives and the decisions we have to make disappears. Right here I need to say something which will help you help other people. If God is a good God, and I am convinced that He is, then His direction is also good.

The one who asks, "What do you think I should do?" may not like the counsel you give (counsel you feel is consistent with the guidelines and principles of Scripture), but if that person accepts the authority of God's Word, there is clear direction.

I am not surprised that people who are committed to the authority of the Word of God often have little faith in secular counseling. In secular psychiatry there is a cacophony of voices competing for dominance, none of which resonates with clarity.

For example, in an experiment Professor D. L. Rosenhan planted eight sane volunteers, one of them a psychiatrist, in eight different psychiatric wards and told them to behave normally. Many of the other inmates immediately recognized that these eight were impostors because their behavior was rational and their conversations meaningful, yet not one staff psychiatrist recognized any signs of normalcy. Said Professor Rosenhan, "Any diagnostic process that lends itself so readily to massive errors of this sort cannot be a very reliable one."[2]

Secular psychoanalysis, which follows the framework first advocated by Sigmund Freud, takes six to eight years on the average and is only partially effective. One-third of all patients undergoing psychoanalysis are eventually "cured," one-third are helped somewhat, and one-third are not helped at all, the same ratio of people who receive no professional help at all.[3]

I should like to make it very clear that I have no ax to grind with modern psychiatry, only with secular forms of treatment and philosophies which are contradictory to the counsel of God's Word, the Bible.

Today there are a growing number of psychiatrists who are committed to the principles of the Word and are using psychiatry as a tool to bring healing to people, like Dr. Ross Campbell of the Southeastern Counseling Center in Chattanooga, Tennessee, and Dr. Frank Minirth and Dr. Paul Meier of the Minirth-Meier Clinic in Dallas. These men have not simply "sprinkled a few verses" over a secular counseling model, but are committed to the authority of Scripture without reservation.

Our word "psychiatry" comes from two Greek words, *psyche* (soul) and *iatria* (healing), and literally means "healing of the soul." The bottom line is that what God says in His Word works—it brings a lasting measure of happiness in life.

Having counseled and worked with people for more than thirty years, I have come to the conclusion that even if I were not a Christian and did not believe in ultimate accountability to God, I would still give the same counsel and direction to people. I am convinced the guidelines which we find in the Word of God are necessary for people to live well-adjusted lives and to find meaning and purpose in living.

For the person who accepts the authority of the Word, believing that it was given by the inspiration of the Holy Spirit, the Bible is not simply one of many different options which may work. It is *the way* to fulfillment and happiness.

The Bible recognizes that man's fundamental problem is estrangement from his Creator, which is labeled as "sin." This old-fashioned and seldom-used word is rarely found in the vocabulary of secular psychology apart from derisive allusions to religions that create guilt.

Some, however, have addressed the issue of sin and how it relates to God and each other. Psychiatrist Karl Menninger of the Menninger Clinic wrote the following in *Whatever Became of Sin?*:

> I believe there is "sin" which is expressed in ways which cannot be subsumed under verbal artifacts such as "crime," "disease," "delinquency," "deviancy." There is immorality; there is unethical behavior; there is wrongdoing. And I hope to show that there is usefulness in retaining that concept, and indeed the word, sin, which now shows some signs of returning to public acceptance. I would like to help this trend along.[4]

Long ago Augustine said, "Thou hast made us for Thyself, O God, and our heart is restless until it finds its rest in Thee." Regardless of how men view it, dealing with sin and estrangement from God and each other is a fundamental issue that the Bible addresses clearly. Critics of the Bible, charging that religion creates guilt by making people feel the issue of sin, fail to recognize that the cross of Jesus Christ provides redemption and forgiveness, thus eliminating the burden of human failure.

Counseling in a Biblical Framework Recognizes the Bible as a Guide for Moral Conduct

Some think of the counsel of Scripture as an impossible dream, something well and good, lofty and noble, but just not practical in our world today. Others think of it as a benchmark, something to strive for, but unrealistic and impossible to attain. I realize that the lives of many believers fall far short of the standard of Scripture, but the fault is not that God has demanded the impossible of us. Rather, we have failed to attain the measure of happiness which He wills.

As G. K. Chesterton once said, "Christianity has not been tried and found lacking; it has been tried and found difficult."

I had just spoken on commitment in marriage, when an attractive, very nicely dressed, middle-aged woman approached me and said, "About your message this morning . . ."

She paused and her face became flushed as she said, "I tried it, ——— it, but it didn't work!"

Somewhat surprised by her bluntness, I asked, "You tried what?"

"Well, I tried to live by the Bible, and it just didn't work!"

The counsel of Scripture works only as you cooperate with God striving to do what He wants you to do. You are not a machine that mechanically does only the will of its inventor; you are a person made in the image of God, with will, sensibilities, and emotions. But most important of all, you were given the tremendous power of choice, and your decisions make the difference as you create your future.

God says, "This is the way to happiness; walk this path," and with that direction comes the power of the Holy Spirit, which enables you to rise above the quicksand of your own sinful nature. The old cry of, "I can't help the way I am," is drowned out by the chorus of those who can say through experience, "I'm a different person because Christ changed my life and put my feet on the solid Rock."

When you help a friend by counseling from a biblical perspective, your approach is that God said what He meant and meant what He said. He neither excuses nor condones our sin or failure, but extends forgiveness and help in overcoming the pull of our old natures. What a person's life is like at the present—either good or bad—isn't the issue; it's what it can become with the help of a loving God who only designs good for His children.

Counseling in a Biblical Framework Recognizes that the Bible Is Not Only Cross-Cultural but Counter-Cultural As Well

We live in a pagan society that constantly bombards us with ideas, attitudes, suggestions, and lifestyles which are out of harmony with the great plan God has for us. The person who is struggling with decisions affecting his future may be strongly pulled by two forces: the flesh and his culture.

The flesh or the old nature often pulls him away from the path of God's will. Remember Paul's struggle with this as he cried out, "For the good that I will to do, I do not do; but the evil I will not to do, that I practice" (Rom. 7:19).

Our culture is the fabric which surrounds our lives, and it's reinforced by the media, our often-fictitious heroes and heroines. We come face to face with our culture as we stagger through the check-out counter at the grocery store wishing we could look like the beautiful people who adorn the covers of the magazines.

You have a friend, Lois. She's a single woman with a good sales position in a growing company. Her boss John has invited her to attend a convention with him in Las Vegas and immediately she said, "Great idea!" She was ready for a little excitement and a change of scenery, but then he told her to make reservations—one room with a double bed. Lois didn't say anything *to him*, but she's troubled.

The boss's secretary said, "Way to work up the corporate ladder!"

Another told her, "What difference does it make; everybody does it these days as long as it's safe."

Lois is a Christian, a single mother who would so much like to find a good husband who could also be a father to her two little boys. Thinking about the weekend and the sexual expectations that go with it, her conscience says, "Hey, you don't want to get tangled up in this; you know it's wrong! This is not for you!" But when she talks to you about the situation, she admits that she feels attracted to him. After all, he's witty, intelligent, and fun, and he makes her feel important, something her ex-husband never did.

That's the pull of the flesh or the old nature; that few have convictions about commitment to one person in marriage these days is culture, and the will of God mitigates against both.

When a person is not a believer in Jesus Christ, you can't expect him or her to have the same viewpoint or maintain the same lifestyle as one of God's children. "The natural man [person] does not receive the things of the Spirit of God, for they are foolishness to him; nor can he know them, because they are spiritually discerned" (1 Cor. 2:14).

Counseling in a Biblical Framework Recognizes
that the Bible Deals in Precept or Principle
with Every Situation in Life

"That's quite a claim!" you may be saying to yourself.

Yet if God's will is not broad enough to give us guidance in all the decisions and choices of life, including the ones which have recently been created by science, culture, and medicine, then God would have left us vulnerable to some of the most pressing and crucial issues confronting men and women today.

God will not leave us in darkness or leave us on our own when it comes to the issues of life. Remember the promise of Jesus: "I am the light of the world. He who follows Me shall not walk in darkness, but have the light of life" (John 8:12).

The Bible gives pointed statements indicating His will when it comes to most of today's issues. For example:

- The kind of person I should marry—2 Corinthians 6:14
- My moral life outside of marriage—1 Thessalonians 4:3
- The way I conduct my business—Romans 12
- Why I should keep my marriage together—1 Peter 3:7

The statements just listed are clear and unequivocal. You may not like what God says, but you understand clearly what He wills. Yet there are many issues that are unique to our times and weren't even thought of when Paul wrote the epistles.

God has not ignored these situations but gives us guidance through principles. Included in this category are issues such as abortion, surrogate mothering, in vitro fertilization, test tube babies, artificial insemination, euthanasia, and so forth.

Whether or not God ever intended us to be confronted with some of those issues is not the question;

we are faced with them, and at some point we have to say, "Yes, I believe this is pleasing to God!" or "No way! I don't think God would approve of this because of the principle we find in Scripture!"

Looking in a concordance under "A" you won't find the word "abortion," but as you search the pages of Scripture you will find statements such as, "For you created my inmost being; you knit me together in my mother's womb. . . . When I was woven together in the depths of the earth, your eyes saw my unformed body. All the days ordained for me were written in your book before one of them came to be" (Ps. 139:13,15,16 NIV).

From this you synthesize a principle: life is a gift from God and is sacred. And this principle gives you personal guidance in the choices which confront you.

Counseling in a Biblical Framework Recognizes
that All Genuine Healing Comes from God.

A fundamental premise of Scripture is that sin separates men and women from God and from each other, but healing produces restoration and harmony. The theme of Scripture is that redemption involves healing—spiritually, emotionally, and, yes, even physically. Through Moses God said, "I am the Lord who heals you" (Exod. 15:26). Through David we learn that God "forgives all my sins and heals all my diseases" (Ps. 103:3 NIV). Jesus went about healing "many who were sick with various diseases" (Mark 1:34). "Wherever He entered, into villages, cities, or the country," reported Mark, "they laid the sick in the marketplaces, and begged Him that they might just touch the border of His garment. And as many as touched Him were made well" (Mark 6:56).

Counseling from a biblical perspective is an extension of the healing ministry of Jesus in the realm of the emotions and the spiritual life; however, there is one more important prerequisite which must be mentioned for you to be an effective counselor and helper of hurting people.

Counseling in a Biblical Perspective Requires a Working Knowledge of the Word of God

"But I am just a layperson!"

"I've never gone to Bible school or a Christian college!"

"Why not just refer people to our pastor! After all, isn't that what we pay him to do?"

"I can't help anybody!"

The chapters which follow will give you a plan which does work. It is simple. Like the Four Spiritual Laws, which have helped thousands to share their faith, the formula which I have developed for laypeople takes the sweat out of helping people.

It works with personal problems, family problems, even business problems. But before you can be effective in helping people, you need to know what the Word says about some of the fundamental issues of life:

- Roles, relationships, and responsibilities in family living
- Sin and guilt
- Forgiveness and restitution
- Fear and the faith that overcomes it
- The place of sex in our lives and marriage

Jay Adams in his book *Competent to Counsel*, which

has become a valued source book for serious Christian counselors, contends that the best possible preparation for counseling is a seminary education. This, however, is impossible for most of you reading this book, and you may be tempted to stop helping people, overwhelmed by your own inadequacy. Or you have another choice: find out what the Bible says about these key issues. Become a "lay specialist."

By the time you finish this book, you will have been exposed to what the Word says about the basic issues people face and that knowledge will give you confidence when the question comes, "What do you think I should do?" You will have some idea how to answer, incorporating the plan of God to bring wholeness to relationships and lives.

Go deeper on your own by marking passages used in this study in your Bible. Make your own cross references in the margin of your Bible; where you know a Scripture verse on a given topic, make a note of another verse which relates to the same issue. Use the blank pages at the end of your Bible to give you some references to use when someone asks for help in working through an issue.

I'll also give you some techniques which will help you be more effective. The formula which we are talking about is this:

Now, let's take the first step—getting started.

2

Getting Started

Today we live in a world of quick fixes, fast foods, and instant replay. We aren't content with waiting for answers tomorrow; we want everything today, right now. A sign in a restaurant reads, "Lord, bless the instant coffee, the one-minute oatmeal, and the pop-up waffles. In haste, Amen!"

When it comes to unraveling difficulties, most folks want immediate, painless solutions. And, of course, such do not usually exist.

The person who has turned to you for help is probably at a fork in the road of life, and the decision or choice which will be made may have consequences which extend far into the future.

Though you hardly need to be concerned about legal implications (unless you counsel professionally or accept money in payment for counseling), you do assume a measure of responsibility for a person's future.

Whenever you say, "I think you should . . ." and finish that sentence, you are potentially the catalyst for change in the entire direction of a friend's life. Dispensing free advice is a serious matter. What you say may keep a friend's marriage together; it may send someone in the direction of a new career; it may even make the difference between life and death for someone who has lost his way.

In the previous chapter I pointed out the fact that we do bear a responsibility before God for each other as part of the family of God—helping, guiding, and encouraging one another. Jesus told the disciples that after He had returned to heaven they would carry on His works and even do greater works than He had done. His words must have been intimidating; nonetheless, they were true.

Today the healing, restoring, helping ministry of Jesus is done through us, His people, His body. That knowledge should not only make you want to better equip and train yourself in helping people, but should also make you more willing to make the sacrifices and take the risks necessary in helping someone else.

Helping People Takes Time

Visualize a case of empty soft drink bottles sitting on your back patio as you water the flowers in your garden. The spray from the hose falls across the small opening of the bottles. A tiny amount of water finds its way into the individual bottles. Not much, but some.

Now, in contrast, visualize taking a bucket of water, and then filling each bottle, one at a time, with a dipper. Takes a lot longer than just spraying the bottles with the hose, right? But the results are thorough.

That's the difference between listening to a pastor's sermon or a Bible study with 200 people present, and talking one-on-one with a friend.

In tennis when someone serves a ball into your court, it's up to you. You may backhand it, use your forehand, smash a volley as hard as you can, or drop an easy shot over the net. But once the ball is in your court, it's your move.

When someone finally gets around to that question, "What do you think I should do?" the ball is in your court. My experience in helping people is that if I am really serious about wanting to help, I've got to be willing to make a commitment of time and emotional energy. I've got to be willing to be involved in the life of that person.

You can, of course, ignore the question and not respond. But the person wouldn't have asked unless he or she was serious about wanting your input. Your failure to respond, or at least to listen, tends to endorse what he or she intends to do. Since you didn't respond otherwise, the person assumes that you are in agreement. It's dangerous.

A pastor came to me and poured out his heart. I listened. I didn't agree with him or his assessment of the situation, but I didn't say so, thinking that we'd talk about it another time. Later I had a rather irate call from one of the deacons in his church saying I had supported the pastor in a dispute.

"Hold on!" I said. "Who said I agreed with him?"

"The pastor!"

My failure was that I listened and didn't respond, which the pastor had interpreted as tacit endorsement.

Failing to follow through when you are asked for help may actually result in doing more to harm a person than to help. If you do not have the time to help someone, or you feel the better part of discretion would be to let someone else help (which may be appropriate when the one who needs help is close to you), or you simply are not qualified, you still must do something to get the ball across the court.

Often taking an hour or even two to talk through a situation is enough. You answered the question or reinforced the voice of conscience with enough fiber that the person could make the right decision. For instance, in the previous chapter I told about Lois, the young woman who was invited to the convention in Las Vegas, and as the result of sharing her heart with a friend she had the courage to go back and say, "I made reservations for *two rooms*. I can do a better job for our company when I'm not emotionally involved even if it's with someone as nice as you."

Often, though, it takes more than one cup of coffee to work through a problem. If your schedule doesn't allow you the time to be involved, it may be necessary for you to say something like, "Look, I really care about you and I sense that this is something really important to you, but it's going to take some time to work through this. I've got to be out of town for the next three weekends, and I think this is too important to wait until I get back. Why don't you talk with (someone you can recommend)?"

But most of the time we sell ourselves short regarding our abilities to help other people. I am convinced that you are far more able to be a positive force for good in the lives of others than you think. I believe this book will give you new insights and tools.

Guidelines for Effective Counseling

The following guidelines are not deeply profound. You might even be tempted to think, "Anybody would know that!" But there are basics, fundamentals which must be observed. Failing to follow through with them hurts our chances of really helping someone.

Even as I am writing this, major league baseball teams have headed for spring training. These are the pros who thrill baseball fans, yet during every spring training the coaches emphasize fundamentals: batting, catching, sliding, timing. Too simple! No, simply necessary.

When You Are Asked, "What Do You Think I Should Do?" Reserve Your Comment Until You Are Certain That You Have the Complete Picture

The greatest single failure of untrained individuals is to jump to conclusions, saying things such as, "Well, it's obvious to me what your problem is . . ." or mentally thumbing through your memorized roster of Bible verses, selecting a couple which seem to have enough weight and then, bang! Hit 'em between the eyes with both of them.

Suppose you say, "Lois, I'm really surprised at you. How would you even consider spending the weekend in Vegas with that jerk who works with you? You've got two kids, and besides, you teach Sunday school. You know better than that!"

What Lois really needs to know is how to handle the situation. She isn't so much interested in going to bed with the guy (she wouldn't have to go to a convention to do that) as she is in knowing how to respond without offending him and preserving her integrity.

But when you come down hard on someone without understanding the situation, you frustrate and even anger the person who has come to you for help. You'll never hear those words, "What do you think I should do?" from that person again.

Simplistic solutions to complex issues offer no real help, either. Quite often when a person comes to me for help, I get the feeling that the person is testing or proving me. The person is sizing me up, thinking, "Can this guy really help me? Should I really unload on him?"

We'll often talk about trivia, then a surface problem, and finally, WHAM! He lets me have it. The real problem!

Had I jumped to a premature conclusion, I would never have had the privilege of helping him work through the real issue. Whether you call it "the problem" and "the real problem," or "surface problems" and "root problems," deep intimate situations of a sensitive nature that may result in embarrassment are not easily addressed. It takes time and confidence in you for a person to be willing to talk about them.

Be Principled as You Handle the Confidence of People

Nothing will hurt a friendship or destroy your credibility faster than breaking confidence with people. It adds insult to injury and bitterness to sorrow. Take, for example, the woman who wrote me about her son in his early 20s who announced that he was gay. The mother went to the pastor of their church and unburdened her heart, telling him the entire story.

The next Sunday, however, the pastor related the whole story in his morning message. He didn't use the boy's name. He didn't have to. The church was fairly small, and that fact made his identity obvious. The mother said, "That has been our home church for more than 20 years, but right now I'd rather take a beating than to go there!"

What do you do when someone includes you in something which has explosive consequences: a teenager is running away from home, a discouraged business colleague is going to take his life, an acquaintance is ripping off the company he works for?

When a person's life is endangered or the consequences of somebody's actions violate the law or seriously affect the lives of other people, you have no alternative but to bring someone else into the picture.

What I recommend is that you convince the person who has come to you that you care, you are a friend, and you love the person so much that you will stand with him or her through this whole situation. Then show the person that other people are necessary to resolve the problem. You may accompany a teenager to the doctor to find out if she is really pregnant. Then when she is convinced that it is in her best interest to bring her mother into the situation, go with her to break the news to Mom.

Knowing that you would be willing to go with a friend to talk to someone about a problem is often enough to help someone make the right decision and begin to work through a problem which has been pushed aside for far too long.

Be Patient with People

Habits that have been many years in the making may not be resolved in a matter of a few minutes. At the same time, however, you have the right to expect change, realizing that the Holy Spirit is the greatest agent of behavioral change the world has ever known. Jay Adams says, "Change for some people is difficult to accept. Change is difficult because change means doing something new, something unusual, something not done before. It usually means exchanging old habit patterns for new ones."[1] Yet growth requires change, and the fact that someone is hurting necessitates change in personal relationships or patterns of behavior. It must come. But it must come with time.

Be Professional

Yes, I know, you are not a professional counselor, but you can value a relationship with someone so much that you treat the confidence he or she has placed in you in a professional manner.

Whenever you reach out to a hurting person of the opposite sex, you run the risk of emotional involvement. You can be concerned with people and at the same time keep your emotions firmly in control. Scores of individuals, though, have listened to someone pour out his or her heart, hearing how a mate had been betrayed. Then as the scalding tears came, the person reached out in a warm embrace to comfort the one being counseled. And from that high voltage emotional situation a compromised relationship developed, eventually leading to the downfall of the marriage of the person who was trying to help.

Let's go back to the situation with Lois. She likes John as a person and admires certain characteristics in his life. She also knows that his constant travel doesn't go over very well with his wife, a rather introverted person who is very content to stay at home.

Lois's refusal to book a room with a double bed—instead of rebuff—brings a profuse and sincere apology. John assures her that he wasn't making sexual advances. He says that he intended it as a joke; Lois doesn't quite believe that, of course. On the two-hour plane ride, John candidly shares some of his frustrations with his marriage, and there's something pathetic in what he says that touches the Madonna part of Lois's psyche.

Because of her emotions, however, she's not the one who should be helping John to work through his personal problems. She is far too apt to become involved herself. She is single and lonely. She's also the personification of what John's wife is not—pretty, nicely dressed, and outgoing.

However some people whose marriages are solid do get emotionally involved in helping others, a danger which only you can evaluate. A warm handshake, direct eye contact, a hospitable cup of coffee or a coke are all ways of conveying warmth apart from physical contact.

Some folks are "huggers," and embracing someone who is hurting is just as natural for them as it is for me to take a hand and shake it warmly. I, for one, advise a certain reluctance when it comes to embracing members of the opposite sex who have come to you for help or counseling. Their emotions may be volatile, and the person you embrace may wish desperately that a mate would do the same thing. When you embrace someone, even though it is in an office setting or even the warmth of your home, your action can trigger an emotional response which is not in the best interest of either of you.

Never counsel a member of the opposite sex when you question your ability to handle a situation. A very prominent pastor was approached by the beautiful wife of one of his deacons for marital counseling. The pastor told her, "Look, you are a beautiful woman and I'm a red-blooded male, and I just don't trust myself to counsel with you!" Shocked? Yes, I was when I heard the pastor relate that story because I know he is a man of God whose ministry is effective. But he knew his weaknesses and openly recognized them.

Most of the time we dispense coffee cup counseling rather informally, perhaps at the office, riding the commuter train home, after a church meeting, or during a lunch break.

After the initial encounter, however, you can have some control over the circumstances. You need a quiet place without interruptions or small children, which may mean you say, "Lois, will you have lunch with me on Thursday? I know a place on 32nd Street where we can have an hour without the phone ringing."

It's O.K. to bring your husband or wife into a counseling situation, especially when you are counseling a member of the opposite sex, by saying, "You know, Bob [your husband] has a lot of insights into how guys think and feel. What would you think about joining us for a cup of coffee Friday night, and we can all talk about this together?"

For your own sake guard against counseling with someone in a place where your integrity could be called into question (such as in a home with someone of the opposite sex when no one else is present, or in a hotel

room). While both of you may be entirely trustworthy
and your willingness to help may be completely honorable, the circumstances don't make the situation look
legitimate, something which Paul warned against (see
1 Thess. 5:22).

Recognize Your Own Limitations

You never lose the respect of someone when you say,
"You know, I'd like to help you with this, but it is more
than I can handle. I'd like to suggest that you see . . ."
(and make a referral to a counselor or a physician).

Don't play medical doctor, either. It's dangerous as
well as unethical. If someone you are working with has
made a commitment to Jesus Christ, and that person
has been under the care of a medical doctor who has
prescribed medication, don't say, "Now that you have
found the Lord, you aren't going to need your medicine anymore!"

Sometimes I am absolutely convinced of that, but I
encourage a person to go back to his or her doctor for
evaluation. Or, if he or she is under the care of a doctor
whose reputation is well known for overmedicating his
patients, I recommend another doctor, one who I know
will take the time to listen to what the patient says instead of merely writing prescriptions. If you know the
doctor personally, you might even want to brief him on
what has taken place.

In Bible Study Fellowship, Barbara became a good
friend with her discussion leader, a warm-hearted, mature woman who reminded her of her own mother.
Joann, the discussion leader, had never thought of herself as a counselor, but the discussions following the

Wednesday studies helped Barbara through a very difficult time in her life when her husband was having an affair with his secretary. But when Barbara's husband filed for divorce and she started talking about suicide, Joann knew that the situation was beyond her. Joann convinced Barbara that she needed help which Joann couldn't give. And she made an appointment with a Christian psychologist in our area, going to the office with Barbara (partly to insure that she kept the appointment).

Telling about it later, Barbara said it was Joann's friendship, not the counsel of the professional, which really brought her through that difficult time of her life and helped her to realize that there is life after divorce. But had Joann failed to reach for additional help and had Barbara taken her life, Joann would have carried a tremendous, unnecessary load for the rest of her life.

Nurture Your Relationship With the Person You Are Helping

Your effectiveness with the person you want to help is determined to a large degree by the relationship you have with that person. Why did your friend come to you initially? Because you are a "nice person"? You just happened to be there? He or she feels comfortable with you? Possibly all three, yet the person struggling with some issue felt you could help, even if it was only by extending a sympathetic, listening ear. Often you help another person a great deal by simply listening— something perhaps no one else has done.

When you counsel with a friend, your relationship is especially important. Proverbs 27:6 notes, "Faithful are the wounds of a friend." A loyal friend is honest. Words of counsel may hurt and even wound, as the writer of Proverbs attested, but those wounds will heal and may prevent a far greater tragedy.

If you tell someone only what he or she wants to hear, your value as a counselor is diminished; on the other hand, if you are so harsh that you drive the person away, your effectiveness is finished.

It is painful for some people to face reality, especially when it doesn't live up to their ideals. An affair falls into that category; it is a temporary, sometimes "make believe" situation which usually terminates in heartache and suffering.

If you are counseling with a couple, you strive to be neutral and objective; yet when issues of right and wrong are at stake, the offending person may feel that you as a counselor have "ganged up" with the offended party. It is important that you make the one you are trying to help feel accepted as a person though you may reject his or her behavior. How is this done?

Relationships that are built on the foundation of respect, trust, and genuine cordiality form bonds that enable you to keep the lines of communication open when the going gets sticky. Your character and integrity give you status and respect in the eyes of other people. Though you may not have thought of yourself in this light, people think of you as "having your act together," meaning they think you can help them get their act together as well.

Before a person runs the risk of becoming vulnerable by telling you where he is hurting, he or she usually asks three questions: Can this person help me? Does he or she care about me? Does this person know what he or she is talking about?

The last question (a matter of knowledge) doesn't cut a lot of ice with most people. Bartenders dispense a lot of advice, but few bartenders have had any training in counseling. If you tend to pontificate or come across as an authority figure who sits in condemnation on the person who turns to you, you're finished.

Genuine, warm concern for people forges lasting relationships that allow you to be an anchor when the storms of life buffet people. Actually, the preparation is done long before you ever hear those words, "What do you think I should do?"

Surely Jesus radiated this kind of warmth to the people who were touched by His life. One of my favorite passages of Scripture speaks of this in the story found in John 8, where the Pharisees shoved a prostitute before Jesus with the scathing words, "The law says, 'Stone her.' What do you say?"

At first Jesus ignored their question, but when they kept asking, "He raised Himself up and said to them, 'He who is without sin among you, let him throw a stone at her first'" (v. 7).

Then Jesus leaned over and began writing on the ground (the only record of Jesus ever writing anything). John doesn't tell us what He wrote, but I've wondered if perhaps he wrote a date on the ground and then looked up at a man who quickly remembered what he had done on that date and slipped away fearful that Jesus would tell what he had done. In all probability the men who seized that girl knew where to find her because they had been in the same place on unofficial business more than once.

As her detractors left, one by one, Jesus said, "Where are those accusers of yours? Has no one condemned you?"

"No one, Lord," she said.

"Neither do I condemn you." What unqualified acceptance!

Then Jesus followed with the words, "Go and sin no more" (John 8:10,11). She knew that Jesus rejected her sin but had accepted her as a person. Some, however, who ask for help are left with the impression that the one to whom they have turned for help is more interested in the lascivious details of their sin than helping him or her overcome it.

A lesson can be learned from the way Jesus handled the conversation with the fallen woman. He knew exactly where she was coming from, yet refrained from asking the questions some would ask, such as:

How did you get into this profession?

How many men do you see every night?

Do you enjoy what you are doing?

Christ didn't focus on the past, but the present ("Where are your accusers?") and the future ("Go and sin no more!"). When you counsel, the real issue is: Where do you go from here and how do you get there?

Rely Totally upon the Lord As You Counsel with People

The person who is a godly counselor and friend prays as he listens. It isn't necessary for you to close your eyes, but it is important to be in an attitude of prayer as you say, "Lord, help me to pick up the silent signals, to read the nonverbal cues, and to hear what is really being said."

The Holy Spirit often gives you intuitive knowledge to ask the right questions, so that the person begins to reveal the real issue.

Now let's see how this works.

3

The First Meeting

Your phone rings and an acquaintance says, "Have you heard about [and the name of a friend of yours is mentioned]?" You haven't, but you get an earful in a few minutes.

"I think you ought to go talk to her about this!" the caller says ending the conversation.

Should you go?

Generally, confrontational counseling is not very successful. I often explain to a person who "sics" me on a friend that there are three things I cannot do: I can't climb a fence that leans toward me, kiss a person who leans away from me, or help someone who doesn't want help.

On occasion I have said, "Look, I understand that you want me to help this person, and I'd like to do that. But until he or she is ready to let me help, I can't do much."

Knowing that a friend is struggling with something, I may arrange for a cup of coffee or lunch simply to let the person know that I am his friend. Spending time together gives the other person an opportunity to open up without letting him know that you have been informed of the problem.

When it is public knowledge that the friend is struggling, you may want to give that person a call and say, "Look, I'm available. If you want to get together and talk, let me know. I'll be there pronto!"

There are times when your phone rings, and you sense a situation is clearly an emergency, and crisis measures are necessary. There are other times when someone does need help, but it isn't a situation that calls for your giving up your evening at home with the family. Setting a time to meet at your convenience may be perfectly appropriate.

Psychologist Clyde Narramore felt strongly about that when his family was at home. One evening the phone rang, and the caller said, "Dr. Narramore, I've just got to talk to you tonight. My marriage is about to fold."

"How old are you?" inquired Narramore.

The caller answered, "Forty-two."

"How many years have you been married?"

"Seventeen years."

"If you are forty-two years of age and have been married for seventeen years, you'll live until morning," said Dr. Narramore. "I'll be happy to see you at the office at nine o'clock."

Most of the time a husband or wife will want to talk with a counselor alone, but if a couple needs help with their marriage and both are willing to come together, I much prefer talking with them together. Why? Each knows what the other has said, and each has an opportunity to clarify the issues.

Unless you hear both sides of the issue, you cannot be certain that the person being described is exactly the one married to your friend. You must understand that what you are hearing is your friend's *perception* of the situation, not necessarily what the situation actually is. The two are often quite different.

Proverbs 18:17 says, "The first to present his case seems right, till another comes forward and questions him" (NIV). Reject the temptation to form a verdict until you hear from both parties.

When you are counseling solo and cannot get the view of the second party in a conflict, you are limited but you can help your friend cope or move in the right direction for help.

Where to Meet

Counseling needs to be comfortable and personal. An office tends to be cold and clinical. A living room usually isn't much of an improvement—too formal. Chairs are too far apart, and it's too structured. By way of contrast, your kitchen table puts you in a warm, friendly environment. It gets you reasonably close to your friend, offers you a place for a cup of coffee or a soft drink, and gives you a surface to write on should you want to make notes.

If you do meet at a restaurant, try to give some thought to its environment. You need quiet and a measure of privacy. I have seen some restaurants which were impossible environments for carrying on meaningful conversations because of the way the tables were placed, and the hustling "get 'em in and out" attitude of the restaurant employees.

I don't recommend this for everyone, but I personally like to make a few brief notes for myself as I listen to someone. At times the friend I am helping will say something significant in passing, and I really want to know more about this. But I also don't want to interrupt the flow of conversation so I'll jot down a word or a phrase, just enough to jog my memory. Later in the conversation, or even the next time we are together, I'll say, "The last time we were together, you said . . . (reminding him or her of the statement). Tell me how you feel about this."

How Often to Meet

How often and for what period of time should you try to see someone? Much of that depends on the nature of the problem which has brought your friend to you for help. Problems which may have been building up over a long period of time are not dispatched with a single cup of coffee or even several, so I often say, "You know, I really appreciate your sharing your heart with me today. I think I can help you work through this, but we need some time to talk, pray, and think. How about making a commitment to get together with me for the next six Wednesdays?"

Or "How about having lunch with me every other week for the next couple of months, and as I get to know you better, I can better answer your questions about . . . ?"

Eventually you will sense that you have taken the person as far as you think you can take him or her. Actually, you are rather pleased that things have gone well and that the issue which first prompted the question, "What do you think I should do?" has been resolved. At that point you may want to say, "I think that you are pretty well on top of the situation. I want you to know that if you need help, I'm available, but I don't think we need to get together on the same, regular basis. Let's set a date for lunch or coffee in two months and talk things over at that time."

What Can Your Friend Expect from You?

The first time I sit down with someone, realizing that the primary purpose of our time together is to work through a problem, I strive to put the person at ease by telling him or her three things. You will want to take these statements and personalize them so that you are comfortable saying them. You need to convey these ideas:

I Will Do Everything in My Power to Help You! But I Cannot Promise an Easy Solution

I often tell people, "I wish I had the ability to look into your heart and say, 'Ah, I see clearly what you need!' I'd write a prescription and send you to the druggist with the assurance that if you take three little white pills in the morning and two blue and green ones in the evening, the problem will go away in four to seven days."

I remind them, "You've got to remember that the intangible problems of the heart are far more difficult than physical problems." I sometimes point out a little scar on my collarbone and tell the person that one day I was showering and felt a little lump. When Dr. Chase saw it, he said, "That's got to come out right now!" It did! A few minutes later I left his office minus the lump and with a bandage marking the spot where the problem had been.

Problems of the heart can't be surgically removed, X-rayed, or submitted to CAT scans for immediate evaluation. Difficulties which may have been in the making for months, or even years, will not disappear in a matter of a few weeks. At the same time assure the friend there *is* a way out, and whether or not you see it at the moment, you will stay with the person until a solution is found. The fact that you have hope gives confidence to a person who may have given up in a relationship.

I Will Keep Your Confidence: You Can Trust Me

The person who comes to you is pretty sure that you are trustworthy, but your making this commitment helps the friend risk being vulnerable enough to tell you exactly what is happening in his life.

Sometimes I say, "When you go to your family doctor, you trust him to keep your confidence, and this is a lot more important than a lump here or there."

On occasion you will be counseling with people in your church, your Bible study, your company, or neighborhood, people with whom you have social contact. It's different from the doctor, whom you first saw garbed in green and in the presence of his nurse, and then meeting him on the street or at a social event.

"Don't you feel funny about knowing certain intimate or personal things about people with whom you have social contact?" you may be thinking. No, not at all.

Some of my best friends (actually many of them) are people that I first got to know in a counseling situation, because of deep personal problems which, in time, were successfully resolved. Today I watch their children growing up and thank God that I had the privilege of helping them make decisions that kept their homes together. The conversations that took place and the situations my friends confronted are a sealed chapter covered with the forgiveness of God and the forgetfulness of real love and friendship.

A word of warning: Resist the temptation to mention a person's problem in your prayer group or Bible study group. "But we need to pray about . . ." Right, I agree. You pray. Pray with the person who needs help, but don't you dare break confidence in the thinly veiled guise of asking for prayer. When my daughter read this section, she penciled a note of sarcasm in the margin of the manuscript: "Christians don't gossip; they just share prayer requests."

Keep confidence with people who trust you enough to open their hearts to you. Your failure to do this is not only a reflection of poor judgment but will ruin your friendship. It destroys your effectiveness as a coffee cup counselor and may diminish the possibility of your friend's resolving his problem.

I Cannot Help You Unless I Know
Where You Hurt

Then, so that my statement doesn't appear to be saying, "Let's hurry up and get on with this; you're wasting my time," I say, "We've got plenty of time. I know that it may not be easy for you to talk about some things, so why don't you start at the beginning and tell me what brought you here for help?"

Some people, however, really don't want help when they ask, "What do you think I should do?" They may be seeking your opinion like a politician asking advice from his constituency. What you think or say doesn't really matter because they have already decided on a course of action. They simply want to add your name to the roster of people who have endorsed their decision, provided you agree.

I have talked with people who had gone to at least a half-dozen other people before me. "Why did you come to me?" I ask, and I usually hear something like, "Well, I didn't like what so-and-so told me."

How do you know when a person is becoming psychologically dependent on you? What do you do with the person who calls you every day and talks for an hour over the phone giving you a word-by-word account of "He said . . ." and "I said . . ." and then "He said . . ."?

Suggestion: Say, "This is so important that we should talk about this in person. Come over to my house Friday morning at ten. We'll have a cup of coffee, and you can tell me all about it." Your friend, though, may be the mother of five and nursing the baby, as well as working part-time in the school cafeteria. She can't be at your house Friday at ten.

In such a case outline a program of positive action, some kind of situation-improvement homework relating to the problem—a book or article which relates to the need of your friend, a pertinent verse of Scripture which you ask your friend to memorize, a tape which you want him or her to listen to.

Then when your friend calls the next time, say, "Before we get into this today, I'd like to ask, 'Have you read the book (or memorized the verse or listened to the tape) I gave you?'" When the answer is, "No," and you sense that the person wants only sympathy, and not help, say, "I can't really be effective in helping you until you read (or memorize or listen to) it. When you do it, call me back and we'll get together."

There's one more issue you will eventually face. When you succeed in helping someone, on occasion, the person you are helping begins to lean on you and becomes emotionally dependent on you. You begin to feel smothered, and you realize it isn't good for the person you are helping either. Symptoms are daily calls, consultations before even the smallest decisions are made, and the constant nod of approval of what the person considers.

When a child learns to walk, a parent offers support and help, but gradually as the child becomes stronger, the parent doesn't have to provide the same help. That is the way it must be with those we counsel. Understanding the goals of counseling and helping a person move toward psychological independence will free both you and him from that dependent relationship. This is the subject of our next chapter.

4

The Counseling Process

When you set out on a journey by automobile and you are unsure of your way, you take a road map, something which can guide you toward your destination. In a very real sense, God has given us a road map for our lives. The Bible gives you some idea of where you should be headed.

When a person has gotten off the right road, and you know the geography, you say, "You can't get where you want to go from here. You need to go back and take another road." When you are familiar with Scripture and can look at a friend's problem objectively, you have some idea of what the person needs to get back on the right track.

Three objectives serve as goals, and though progress never takes a straight line, you move toward them as you would geographic landmarks in the distance. You can observe progress in getting back to the right road as you pass through these phases of the helping process. The following diagram may help you see what I'll be discussing in the rest of the chapter.

THE THREE GOALS OF COUNSELING
1) Identify the problem

2) Analyze the available options and the consequences of accepting or rejecting each one
3) Help your friend discover and choose the will of God for his life

The counseling process is like a time-line through which a person must pass if a problem is to be effectively resolved.

The Counseling Process

GOALS:	1) Identify the problem	2) Analyze the available options	3) Discover and choose God's will
PHASES:	EXPLORATION	ENCOUNTER	RECONSTRUCTION
COUNSELOR'S ACTION	Listens Evaluates Questions Ponders	Establishes responsibility through questions	Guides through repentance & reconstruction

As you work through a given problem with someone, you will find that these three phases of the counseling process are not marked by specific boundaries any more than the passing from youth to middle age. But the process involves a transition which is necessary to resolve the problem.

Phase 1—Exploration

During this period you listen, evaluate, question, ponder. Like a physician who examines a patient for the first time, you are trying to get the picture clearly. You understand that initially the person who comes to you for help is deciding if you can be trusted. At the same time, his or her feelings may be all mixed up. Life doesn't come to us in neat little packages, and you may get the story in bits and pieces.

This first phase of counseling may take an hour or two, or several weeks. After all, you may be the first person that your friend has ever talked this problem over with, and as you listen, you may only gradually begin to see the picture develop. You have to see the problem clearly before you can help your friend look for solutions. The first phase of counseling relates very closely to goal 1—identifying the problem. This is such a critical part of the counseling process that we will talk about how to accomplish this in this chapter and the one to follow.

Phase 2—Encounter

Once the problem is clearly identified in your mind, you want to help your friend to see the options and the consequences of accepting or rejecting each one. It is in this phase that both of you really come to grips with the issue. This leads to the final leg of the journey.

Phase 3—Reconstruction

At the beginning of this phase, the person you are helping makes a decision. From the options, he accepts the fact that God does have direction for him or her and that this is the path that needs to be taken regardless of how easy or difficult it may be. Here your big task is to provide loving support and help your friend follow through with the decision which has been made. When the one who has come for help is strong enough and mature enough to handle the problem alone, you have worked yourself out of a job.

Now let's go deeper in considering how to help the person who has turned to you for help.

The First Goal of Counseling: Identify the Problem

You may be thinking, "Isn't the problem really obvious?" What may be totally obvious *to you* may not be obvious at all to the person you are trying to help. And what may be obvious to him may not be at all clear to his wife or girlfriend. Long ago the wise man who penned Proverbs 16:2 recognized this as he wrote, "All the ways of a man are pure in his own eyes . . . ." The word translated "pure" in the *New King James Version* also means, "upright" or "just."

Quite often we tend to magnify the faults of others and minimize our own; when a problem occurs we tend to see ourselves in a different light than others do. Actually, there are three perspectives which confront the person you are helping—how he sees himself, how his mate or the other person sees him, how God sees him.

Believe me, experience gained through many years of counseling and working with people has convinced me that these three seldom match up. Until the person who has come for help gains these three perspectives, he will not see the necessity of moving into the second phase of counseling. Let me illustrate.

Jack and Michelle have been married for eighteen years. He's forty and she is thirty-eight. When they got married, she weighed 103 pounds and had a perfect hourglass figure. Now, approaching their middle years, everything has changed. He's obviously out of shape, and Michelle has added more weight than she would care to admit.

When they were first married, they had a tough time financially. During Michelle's difficult first pregnancy, they both became believers in Jesus Christ and joined a church. Michelle volunteered to help in the church nursery, taking her turn along with the other young mothers, and Jack often attended the men's fellowship, especially when his fishing buddy, Pete, offered to take him.

To supplement their income, Michelle soon went to work. Because Jack was an electrical engineer, his income rose, but so did his responsibilities. When babies two, three, and four came along, Michelle's income was an absolute necessity. Michelle's life was filled with activities—church, PTA, new computer programs at work. When Jack was promoted to management, he began traveling at least one weekend out of four. With Jack away from home, or else buried in his den catching up with paperwork, their marriage seemed to sink into the morass of middle-age boredom.

At first there wasn't anything really wrong, apart from the fact that flatness had taken the edge off their relationship. When they were together, they either had nothing to say or else picked at the little things they didn't like about each other.

There were a lot of things that Michelle wanted to say about the two of them, and she so much wanted to walk hand in hand together as they used to do at the beach. She yearned to have those quiet times they had when they were first married and had nothing but each other, when night after night they would sit on the old, worn rug in front of the fireplace and pour out their hearts.

She would like to say, "Jack, remember how you used to run your hands through my hair and tell me I was the most beautiful girl you ever saw? You never do that any more."

Lost in the passing of time was the intimacy which meant so much—the complete honesty and openness they once had with each other. She remembered the time she was afraid to get a Novocain shot at the dentist, and instead of just saying, "That's dumb! Nothing to be afraid of," Jack took off an hour early from work and went to the dentist with her. But all of that was history.

One day she interrupted the Dodgers game as she blurted out, "Jack, if you weren't so addicted to that stupid TV, you might have time for me and your kids." Adding insult to injury, Jack said, "All right, what do you want?"

She tried to communicate her feelings, but she got brilliant responses like, "Yeah. Sure. Why not? I couldn't care less."

She felt rejected and hurt.

When Michelle later brought up the possibility of professional counseling, Jack was irate. "I don't need to talk to some shrink. Our marriage is as good as those airheads who think they know it all and charge us eighty-five dollars an hour. And besides, if we can't make it work, nobody can do it for us."

Within six months Michelle had gained another ten pounds and had joined a weight-loss group, but nothing really seemed to help. And Julie was hired as Jack's new secretary.

A divorcee with two small children, Julie was trim and pretty like Michelle had been in the early years of their marriage. Jack didn't say anything but he noticed.

"You know my wife is always complaining because . . . well, she says I'm a lousy communicator, and I suppose she's right," Jack said one day as he finished a dictation session.

"Nonsense," Julie replied. "I've found you to be interesting, informative, and . . . well, nice."

"Really?" Jack commented with warmth.

That's how it started. But after that, conversations became longer and more intimate. Eventually Julie told Jack how her husband had walked out on her and left her for someone more exciting, and Jack began to share how flat his marriage had become.

At first it was just talk—nothing more. But without realizing it, Jack began to think up excuses to spend more time with Julie—working on the end-of-the-year report at night or having dinner together planning the convention.

But it all changed the night Julie dropped a piece of paper on the floor at the side of the desk. As she leaned over to pick it up, her long brown hair fell against his cheek. Without thinking Jack pulled her face close to his and kissed her.

Instead of pulling away, Julie said, "You shouldn't have done that. But it sure felt good. It's been so long since someone did that to me." It was only a matter of days until the convention in Chicago just happened to find them with hotel rooms side by side, but the maid had to change only one set of linen.

For six months Michelle didn't even consider the fact that she was sharing her husband with someone else. When Jack joined a gym and lost fifteen pounds, she just assumed that he had started out on a new health kick. He still went to church occasionally and seemed more engrossed in his work than ever before.

When Michelle finally learned about Jack's affair, she was crushed and very angry. There were tears and harsh, angry words—plenty of them. Both accused the other of being the real problem.

"Let's talk to Pastor Jack at church!"

"No way! We're not washing our dirty linen in front of other people."

Jack was torn. At times he didn't know his own feelings. Sometimes he regretted what he was doing, especially when he picked up his three-year old, who had fallen asleep on the couch. He remembered how he and Michelle had prayed so hard together when she was six months pregnant and it looked like she was going to lose the baby.

Lying in bed at night hearing Michelle sob in her sleep, he knew he was really hurting her. He wouldn't admit it, but in the quietness of the night, he knew God was saying, "Hey, this is not what you really want, nor what I want. What you're doing is wrong. You've come too far, and I've helped you too much already to blow it. Straighten out your life. Get help!"

Jack's work was affected too. He couldn't concentrate. The picture of Michelle and the kids was still on his desk; but Julie was just outside his office door at her desk . . . and available.

The next weekend was the opening of fishing season, a ritual he and his old fishing buddy Pete had observed since they were kids. No way was he going to miss this one.

It was the evening of opening day when he and Pete were up at the fishing lodge in Wisconsin. They sat in front of the old stone fireplace and began to talk. After swapping yarns about the "big ones" they used to catch, Pete finally said, "Hey, Jack, got something on your mind? You seem as nervous as a cat in a room full of rocking chairs."

It all came out that night, every bit of it, how their marriage had grown stale, how Michelle had gained weight and kept complaining, and how beautiful and available Julie was. At two o'clock in the morning the question finally came: "Pete, you seem to have your head screwed on pretty straight. What do you think I should do?"

What Jack would never, ever have done with a professional, he did with a friend with whom he felt comfortable—he opened his heart and sincerely reached for help! What a tremendous opportunity for Pete, the fishing buddy who often took Jack to the men's fellowship at church!

Now as a friend and a counselor, Pete's first task is to help Jack see himself *as he really is,* then to help him see himself from Michelle's viewpoint (and possibly the perspective of his kids, ages three to eight, as well), and most importantly, to help him see himself as God sees him.

How Is This Accomplished?

Through penetrating questions! If Pete is to be effective as a counselor-friend, he's got to help Jack see the full picture.

It isn't difficult for Pete to get the picture of how Jack views himself. He sees himself as a red-blooded male with sexual needs that are not properly being met in his marriage. He tells Pete how repulsive it has become to make love with a woman who is sixty pounds overweight and constantly nags at him.

He also believes that what he is doing isn't so bad. "After all," he reminds Pete, "everybody is doing it these days, even preachers . . . ," justifying himself as he launches into a tirade against a local pastor who ran off with the church organist.

He further sees no wrong in his spending time and money on Julie. "I haven't hurt my kids or Michelle," he tells Pete.

How does Michelle see him? She sees him as a traitor to his vows, as an adulterer who cheated on her, and as a thief who has taken money and gifts which should have been hers and their children's, giving them to his secretary.

How does God view what has taken place?

When I am working through a situation like this with someone, I often ask, "How do you think God feels about what has happened?" Answers are usually trite, like, "Oh, I think He understands; after all, He made me the way I am." Or "I don't know; I never thought much about it."

At this point I say, "Let's take a look at what God says about our lives in this book, the Bible."

I should point out that what the Bible says is in conflict with some theories which are embraced in secular counseling disciplines. Before I describe the four major secular counseling models, let's make sure we understand what God does say about responsibility.

The Bible stresses individual, personal responsibility.

From the very beginning of time, mankind has sought to blame someone else, or circumstances over which he had no control, for his failures. Remember that Adam evaded responsibility for taking the fruit by blaming Eve, "The woman whom You gave to be with me, she gave me of the tree, and I ate" (Gen. 3:12).

Adam was saying, "Look, God, it's partly Your fault because *You* put her here in the garden with me, and *she* took the fruit. All *I* did was innocently eat it." His reply to God's question about eating the fruit was a far cry from the truth, "Yes, I took the fruit of my own volition, and I am completely responsible for my actions!"

A passage which I almost always use to establish personal responsibility is Ezekiel 18:20–23,

> The soul who sins shall die. The son shall not bear the guilt of the father, nor the father bear the guilt of the son. The righteousness of the righteous shall be upon himself, and the wickedness of the wicked shall be upon himself.
>
> But if a wicked man turns from all his sins which he has committed, keeps all My statutes, and does what is lawful and right, he shall surely live; he shall not die. None of the transgressions which he has committed shall be remembered against him. . . . Do I have any pleasure at all that the wicked should die?" says the Lord GOD, "and not that he should turn from his ways and live?

When it comes to infidelity in marriage, several Scripture passages speak clearly. You need to know where these are and be able to turn to them. Note the following passages: "It is God's will that you should be holy; that you should avoid sexual immorality; that each of you should learn to control his own body in a way that is holy and honorable, not in passionate lust like the heathen . . ." (1 Thess. 4:3–5 NIV).

Jesus denounced adultery, as recorded in Matthew 5:27–30 and 19:3–10, emphatically saying that if a man even lusted after a woman, he had committed adultery with her in his heart. (Also see Mark 10:1–12 and Luke 16:18 for parallel renderings.)

People often blame their physical chemistry, as Jack did: "I can't help doing what I do because God made me the way I am!" They blame the environment or society. They explain away their conduct, excusing themselves because of social pressures. But God says *you are responsible for what you do!*

Another passage which is often helpful to establish moral responsibility is the story of David and Bathsheba. God sent the prophet Nathan to David to confront him with the enormity of his sin. Nathan told a story about two men, a rich man who had flocks and herds, and a poor man who had only one little ewe lamb, which was his children's pet. The rich man seized the poor man's lamb, killed it, and prepared a meal for a traveler who had come to him. David burned with anger and vowed that the man who did this must surely die. "Then Nathan said to David, 'You are the man!'" (2 Sam. 12:7).

Establish responsibility by asking questions. Yes, you can tell someone how wrong they are or what a stupid thing they have done and generate a considerable amount of guilt (or anger), but what you want to do is help the person *accept* the full responsibility of his actions.

Undoubtedly, David had pondered the circumstances surrounding his affair, but he had tried to keep it quiet. God (through Nathan) said, "You did it secretly, but I will do this thing before all Israel, before the sun," (2 Sam. 12:12). Once David had taken the step of passion, there was no turning back. He didn't intend for the nation to know that he had engineered the death of a faithful and honorable man so he could take that man's wife to bed.

It hit him with a tremendous impact!

"I have sinned against the Lord," cries David. His repentance and deep sorrow for what he had done were sincere. David tells of his remorse and anguish in Psalm 51. He cries, "I acknowledge my transgressions, and my sin is ever before me. Against You, You only, have I sinned, and done this evil in Your sight . . ." (v. 3,4). At this point David saw himself as God saw him, as he really was, and as others saw him. Only then was he prepared to face the implications of what he had done and experience the reconstruction process that followed.

In helping Jack see himself from God's perspective, Pete eventually has to focus on how God looks at the situation.

Pete could say something like, "You know, Jack, I remember a situation in the Bible where someone worked himself into a corner, kind of like you've done. Let's take a look at it together," and then go to that passage.

Pete can ask penetrating questions such as these:

"As painful as David's sin may appear, do you think God views what you have done any differently? How does God view what's taken place?"

Identifying the Problem Leads to Accepting the Responsibility

Dr. Frank Pittman is a psychiatrist who specializes in

why people become involved in relationships outside marriage. In his book *Private Lies: Infidelity and the Betrayal of Intimacy,* Pittman tells of interviewing 100 couples who describe in detail why they got involved with someone else. "It was not sex but a lack of intimacy that had compelled them to have an affair," says Pittman.[1]

What Jack and Michelle once had, what she desperately wanted again, was intimacy—commitment, mutual trust, openness, total honesty, and vulnerability as both were absolutely transparent with each other. Jack's lack of communication made him distant and less intimate.

Marriage is a husband and wife's commitment to try to meet each other's needs, and those needs go far beyond sexual needs. While most men think only in terms of environmental needs (food, shelter, and clothing), a woman's needs are far more complex.

Jack had never considered the fact that Michelle's needs include communication, intimacy, and a feeling of self-worth. His comments about her weight (her trips to the refrigerator had become a reaction against his lack of communication, which became a vicious circle) did nothing to improve her self-image. Remember when they were first married he often told her how beautiful she was.

A man who accepts responsibility for his family must also make provision for the needs of his wife just as she must meet those same needs in her husband. Paul had strong words for husbands who give little thought to the needs of their wives: "If anyone does not provide for his own . . . he has denied the faith and is worse than an unbeliever" (1 Tim. 5:8).

When needs are not met, our sexual lives are first to be negatively affected, and when a reluctant or insecure partner does not meet the sexual needs of a mate, a vacuum is created that another person may satisfy.

When I sense that this situation may exist, I ask, "Could you have been partly responsible for your mate's actions by your indifference? By failing to meet his or her sexual needs? By a lack of interest in his or her world?" Or, "Have you attempted to view this situation from your husband's or wife's perspective? Tell me honestly—what would you have done if you had been in his or her shoes?"

Meeting each other's needs is vital. A few years ago a young man named William Glasser was in medical school preparing to become a psychiatrist. He began to reject many of the premises of modern psychiatry, especially Sigmund Freud's theory of psychoanalysis. By the time Glasser finished his evolution of thought, he had pioneered a new approach to meeting the needs of people which he called "reality therapy" (his book bears this title).[2] Apart from organic illnesses, such as schizophrenia, Glasser says that there is no such thing as mental illness. He contends that mental illnesses such as neurosis and psychosis are but masks or symptoms of irresponsibility.

Glasser believes that every person—whether a gray-haired grandmother or a tiny baby—has two basic needs: the need to love and be loved, and the need to feel worthwhile to one's self and to other people. When these needs are met, believes Glasser, people act in a responsible fashion. When those needs are not met, irresponsibility, often labeled as mental illness, results.

Glasser, a Roman Catholic by faith, doesn't attempt to correlate what he believes with what the Bible teaches, yet those two needs—love and fulfillment—are definitely within the broad framework of what the Bible says about our lives. The Bible, however, goes beyond these in asserting that every person has a third need—the need for security, which is met through a vertical relationship with God.

Glasser would advise Julie against a relationship with Jack—not because God views it as sin—but because her needs cannot be met in a casual affair.

Along with Glasser many other psychiatrists today are also saying what the Word of God has been saying for centuries: "You are responsible, and you can change," though most of them do not accept the biblical concepts of sin and redemption.

One of the newest voices is that of British psychiatrist Garth Wood, who contends that neurosis is a myth. He says "moral therapy" is the cure for people who suffer because they have violated their own ethics, meaning you stop blaming the environment or illness or other people and begin reflecting on your inner values (whatever they may be). Wrongdoing, in Wood's view, is not the violation of the laws of God, but rather the violation of your moral system, which effectively eliminates any objective criteria of morality or right and wrong. Wood's approach is pragmatic—if it gives you relief, it must be right.

Of course, I don't agree with that premise; the Bible lays down very clear moral guidelines, and God has commanded us to serve others, not ourselves.

The Second Goal of Counseling: Analyze the Available Options and the Consequences of Accepting or Rejecting Each One

During the first phase of counseling you are trying to get the picture, but seeing the picture clearly doesn't change anything. You have to move into the second phase: encounter.

Here you want to explore the available courses of action. You must confront your friend with the consequences of his or her action, as hard as it may be to face them. The past ceases to be important. The future is everything, and the present decides what the future will be.

Don't let this one slide or pass over it casually. It's important because failure to recognize the consequences of our actions will result in default. We then bear the natural consequences, which in Jack's case would probably be a divorce. When we refuse to recognize the consequences, right or wrong, we live with the results of poor choices.

The big question with which you must confront your friend is this: *"Where do we go from here? What plan do you have?"*

The question is usually greeted with a response of, "I don't know!"

Then I ask, "What options do you see? Let's start making a list of the options, and then, once we have the list, let's consider what would happen with each choice."

In Jack's situation, he has three:

1) He can do nothing at all.

2) He can ignore Michelle's objections and continue to see Julie on the side.

3) He can break off the relationship with Julie, which probably means finding a new secretary as well.

You can usually come up with the options yourself but don't do it. You want your friend to face the options him- or herself, and, even more importantly, to recognize what is going to happen as the result of his choice.

What Are the Consequences of These Options?

Once Jack listed his options, I would move on to the next question: What are the consequences of each?

1) Choosing to do nothing at all is the choice to continue to see bitterness and resentment destroy his relationship with Michelle. At times I remind people that they may start over, but they never start again. I remind them of their first kiss, the purity of their love, their first child, and the joy they experienced in sharing what little they had together.

A powerful consideration Jack needs to face is the impact of his affair on his children. Dr. Paul Popenoe, a long-time authority on the American family, contends that when a couple have two children, the lives of at least 12 people are affected: the couple who agree to disagree, the parents of each spouse, the two children who grow up with inadequate emotional and financial support, and even *their* children when they marry. What happens between two people in a marriage vitally affects the future of everyone in the family circle.

If Jack chooses to ignore this issue, he is making a decision to see his family disintegrate further. Prodding deeper I'll ask, "Is this situation good?" Then I will turn to James 4:17 and ask Jack to read it out loud. It says, "To him who knows to do good and does not do it, to him it is sin."

If the point hasn't already been clearly established, right here it is necessary to label this situation what it is in the sight of God—sin! If God views the affair as sin, and Jack recognizes it as such, then the door opens for forgiveness and healing.

2) He can ignore Michelle's objections and continue to see Julie on the side. But trying to put distance be-

tween the two women inevitably compounds the problem. Proverbs 28:13 says, "He who covers his sins will not prosper, but whoever confesses and forsakes them will have mercy."

If, however, the mate doesn't know what is happening (and, on occasion you will talk with someone whose husband or wife isn't aware yet of what is going on), your friend faces the consequences of living a life of deception, covering his or her tracks, and postponing eventual discovery.

This person's situation is much like the youth who had borrowed his father's car without permission. As he was returning from his joy ride, he failed to see a car coming from a side street and ran into the other car, damaging the front of his father's car. As he stood beside the crumpled fender, he closed his eyes and said, "Dear God, I pray this didn't happen!"

There is no way you can unscramble scrambled eggs. Certain actions carry inevitable consequences, some of which are painful. Leaving one woman for another does not eliminate the responsibility a man has to his children, regardless of the failure of the other parent. Jack fathered those children, and he bears a responsibility to and for them.

3) He can break off the relationship with Julie and go to work on his relationship with Michelle. This takes us to the final goal of counseling.

The Third Goal of Counseling: Help the Counselee to Discover and Choose the Will of God for His Life

In the second phase of the counseling process, the issue of wrongdoing must be faced. Glossing over sin, or excusing it on the basis of our human weakness, offers no hope for removing it and overcoming it. But acknowledging it—calling it what it really is—opens up the path of restoration, which is the third phase of the counseling process.

As you analyze the consequences of the options, you then have to bring the one you are helping to a place of confrontation with the will of God. Obviously, it cannot be the will of God for a person to continue in any sinful relationship or situation.

The concept behind the Greek word *hamartia,* usually translated "sin" in the New Testament, is that of missing the mark, of falling short of the target. Acts of wrongdoing have taken your friend outside of God's will. To right the wrong requires positive action, which means breaking habits that have become comfortable and perhaps enjoyable.

At this point the relationship you have with your friend is tremendously important. Sometimes simply being there—encouraging, loving, and reinforcing without condemnation—is the additional strength that a person needs to do the right thing, especially when your friend *knows what is right* but lacks the courage to take the first step toward the will of God. Many Christians whose marriages fail fall into this category, and the input of a coffee cup counselor could have made the difference in helping to restore a troubled marriage.

What is Necessary to Bring Healing to a Broken Relationship?

The process of reconciliation can be thus illustrated:

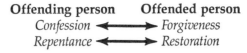

Offending person **Offended person**
Confession ◄────► *Forgiveness*
Repentance ◄────► *Restoration*

In an old fishing lodge as the sun was coming up over the horizon, Pete and Jack knelt and prayed together. Jack wept tears of repentance. He freely confessed that he didn't know how his marriage with Michelle would come together, but he knew he had to ask Michelle's forgiveness and ask her to try one more time. Instead of going fishing, the two men drove home, and a tearful reunion with Michelle followed.

How much should someone like Jack tell the one who has been offended and hurt?

Confession of sin before God and the one who has been hurt is necessary, but a recital or cataloging of transgressions before the offended party is not necessary. I do not believe that every morbid detail has to be reviewed in the presence of a mate. God knows already, and the husband or wife knows that he or she has been betrayed.

Jack needs to know that God will forgive him and remove the sin. (See such passages as Psalm 51, Isaiah 43:25, Psalm 103:12, and 1 John 1:9.)

Once the sin has been confessed, it is necessary for the offending spouse to ask forgiveness of the one he or she has hurt. It is always a joy to pray with someone who confesses his wrongdoing before the Father and then does the same before his mate. And for healing to take place it is essential for the one who has been hurt likewise to extend complete forgiveness.

It is never enough for the offending person to say, "I have done [whatever] and I am sorry that I have hurt you." He or she must also ask, "Will you forgive me for what I have done to you?" The transaction is not complete until the one who has been hurt says, "Yes, I will forgive you."

A couple came to me for counseling with a problem which was serious—very serious. The husband was trying to remodel the kitchen, and his wife didn't much care for the plans. Being under a great deal of stress at work, and at the same time thinking he was bending over backward to do the work on the kitchen, the husband became angry at his wife's objections. He forgot that she was the one who would spend many hours in the remodeled kitchen. In a display of anger he doubled up his fist and let her have it. (Though I can understand the anger, I can never justify physical violence in marriage.)

"Has this happened before?" I asked the husband. He hesitated a bit and then told me this was the first time. But when I asked the wife the same question separately, she said it had happened before, but she couldn't remember how many times.

"Have you ever forgiven him?" I asked.

"Not really! I'm finished. I just can't take this any longer," she replied.

I began working first with him, then with both of them. Eventually he came to understand that stress must be handled apart from allowing his anger to spill over on her or the children. With tears in his eyes, he asked, "Honey, will you forgive me?"

She hesitated, and quietly responded, "Yes, I forgive you."

Later that wife told me, "You know, something changed inside when I said, 'Yes, I'll forgive you.' I had never really forgiven him before, even though he said he was sorry. This time it was different!"

I repeat: *it is necessary for the offending person to ask for forgiveness and just as important for the offended person to extend forgiveness.*

Repentance must also be met with reconciliation, or restoration. No matter how repentant the offending person may be, if the offended party will not really extend restoration to that person, genuine healing cannot take place; the wound continues to fester and will eventually destroy a relationship.

It is very easy for the offended person to remind his or her mate of the wrongdoing. Yes, I understand that once the wall of trust has been broken down, rebuilding it is a long and painful process. But it must be undertaken.

For a long time after the relationship with Julie ended, whenever Jack was late coming home, or had to be out of town, or received a phone call from an unidentified person of the opposite sex, the memories of his affair replayed in Michelle's mind. Jack understood that and did his best to let her know when he expected to be late and why, and Michelle had to remind herself that forgiveness isn't complete when we hold on to bitter memories and let them erode our peace of mind.

Shortly after his eventful fishing trip with Pete, Jack encouraged Julie to find work elsewhere, and Michelle took that as a real sign of commitment to their marriage. Though some of Michelle's friends told her she was a fool to stay with Jack—and at times, she really questioned whether it was the right thing to do—in her heart she realized she had so much to gain by striving to forgive and rebuild.

Writing to the Ephesians about the importance of forgiveness, Paul used the analogy of God's forgiving us as a pattern which we must follow in forgiving each other. "Be kind one to another, tenderhearted, forgiving one another, just as God in Christ also forgave you" (Eph. 4:32).

Jesus said, "For if you forgive men when they sin against you, your heavenly Father will also forgive you. But if you do not forgive men their sins, your Father will not forgive your sins" (Matt. 6:14,15 NIV). Strong words? Why does God demand so forcibly that we forgive each other? Surely the answer must be the high cost which He sustained in giving His son to be crucified at Calvary, providing a means for Him to forgive us.

Maintaining a "holier than thou" attitude destroys the restoration process, and often results in further infidelity.

The day after I had spoken at a certain Bible school, a tearful young woman telephoned me. "I heard you speak yesterday," she began, "and I desperately need your help." She said her husband was preparing for the ministry, and that at the same time he was making a hell of her life.

She said, "When I was a teenager, I had sex with my boyfriend, and then I found the Lord as my Savior and realized that what we were doing was wrong, and I broke it off. Then just before we were married, I felt that I had to tell my fiance that I was not a virgin and confess what had happened."

Sobbing, she said, "But now that we're married he wants more details, and I've told him everything there is to tell. He yells at me saying, 'You're no good; you aren't worthy of me; you are nothing but a slut!'"

"Would you have your husband call me tomorrow?" I asked.

The next day the young man called me. I began to talk about forgiveness and accepting each other because God has forgiven us, but I got nowhere.

Finally I said, "Suppose that I had a machine that could read your thoughts, and that I brought it to your church on Sunday and flashed every thought you have had this past week on a screen for everyone to see, would you be embarrassed?"

I had him and he knew it! He admitted that he would.

Then I shared the words of Jesus who said, "You have heard that it was said to those of old, 'You shall not commit adultery.' But I say to you that whoever looks at a woman to lust for her has already committed adultery with her in his heart" (Matt. 5:27,28).

"Not only would you be ashamed, you would crawl under the nearest chair and hide your face in shame, right?"

He admitted it!

To say, "O.K. I'll forgive you this time but if you ever do it again, we're through!" isn't forgiveness. It is merely probation, and probation is not the same as restoration.

Forgiveness involves God, the offended, and the offending. All three areas must come together for real healing to take place.

In Jack and Michelle's case, real forgiveness and healing took between six months and a year.

Pete was a tremendous help to both Jack and Michelle in the year that followed Jack's tearful confession. Pete was enough older than Jack to counsel him as a "father figure," and he and Jack began meeting weekly to work through the process of healing the broken relationship. Jack agreed to be accountable to Pete, confronting the issues and slowly reconstructing his marriage.

What happened to Jack and Michelle was painful and rebuilding the relationship didn't come easy; but it did come. And looking back on the process, both would tell you, it was the best decision they ever made.

Before we turn the page and begin a new chapter, I'd like to close on a positive note. Though, as Jack Pittman has observed, "Infidelity is the primary disrupter of families, the most dreaded and devastating experience in a marriage, and the most universally accepted justification for divorce," unfaithfulness doesn't have to end in divorce.[3] When people will forgive each other, seek God's healing power, and rebuild the bridges of communication, a broken marriage can be helped. It happened to Jack and Michelle.

5

*Diagnose the Problem
but Treat the Whole Person*

A little bit of knowledge is a dangerous thing! Thirty years ago I had answers for most of life's problems, but looking back from the perspective of several decades of experience, I'm not sure that I even understood the questions. Life is complex, and many of the problems which confront us defy simplistic, "Here's what-to-do-in-three-easy-steps" solutions.

Perhaps the greatest danger confronting those of you who want to help people is that you leap to conclusions as to what people's problems are before you have given them an adequate chance to get to the bottom of their troubles.

I am reminded of the young man who finished his degree in psychology and opened his office. Having put up the sign out front, he was waiting for the world to beat a path to his door. On the third day he heard the sound of footsteps coming down the hall. Intent on impressing his first client with his wisdom, he picked up the phone and said, "Yes, umm-huh! I'm sure I can handle that problem. Yes, indeed. I see patients with that difficulty almost every day. Right! Friday at four. First office down the hall on the right! See you then."

Putting the phone down, he looked up at the young

man standing in front of him and asked, "What can I do for you?"

"I've come to hook up your phone!" replied the visitor.

In the first phase of counseling, the exploratory phase, you, as counselor-friend, are trying to get a handle on what the issue really is. Our tendency is to isolate the spiritual problem—whatever it may be—nailing it to the floor with a Bible verse or two when, actually, the problem is a combination of the emotional, the physical, and the spiritual. Our task would be much easier if we could really deduce that all the problems requiring counseling were spiritual in nature and find Bible verses to neutralize the acid of discontent.

Consequently, we tend to put life in neat little boxes which we label as "emotional problems," "physical problems," or "spiritual problems." One of the first

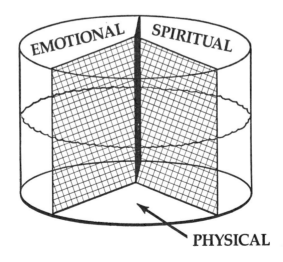

things you must learn, however, is that when someone suffers, though the primary cause may be more directly related to a particular one of these three areas, *all three are going to be affected.*

When the level begins to drain in the honeycomb of life, it sinks in all three areas. I often use the illustration of a cylinder which is divided in three sections by a wire mesh, thus liquids which fill it cannot be kept isolated from each other.

One of my complaints with secular psychiatry is that it fails to recognize the spiritual nature of mankind. Genesis 2:7 says, "And the Lord God formed man of the dust of the ground, and breathed into his nostrils the breath of life; and man became a living being." Made in the image of God, man—even fallen man—has sensitivities and insights possessed by none other of God's remarkable creatures.

Psychiatrists who practice their faith, of course, are in a much different position and recognize that man is a complex composite of the emotional, the physical, and the spiritual.

How Does Psychiatry Treat the Problems of People?

Today psychiatry practices one or more of the following basic forms of treatment:

Shock Therapy

Widely used a few years ago, this form of treatment is no longer (thank God!) used so extensively. Its success has been widely disputed, and the risk of potential damage to the brain is considerable.

Chemical Therapy

The watchword here is "better living through chemistry." Pharmaceuticals have become a major industry, with vast sums of money being spent for tranquilizers and a rainbow of drugs to elevate moods, suppress troubled feelings, or regulate emotions.

I recognize how important and helpful these drugs, on occasion, may be. Some, for example, who suffer depression can find great relief with small doses of lithium, which appears to balance a chemical deficiency in their body, just as glasses correct astigmatism of the eyeball. My objection, however, is to doctors who sedate and tranquilize all forms of problems instead of going to the bottom of the conflict.

Verbal Therapy

Often called "talking cures," psychotherapy covers a wide spectrum of counseling. In a sense those who practice what I call "bibliotherapy" (applying the principles of Scripture to the needs of men and women) are practicing verbal therapy.

Surgery

In severe cases of mental illness, neurosurgery is a last resort.

Diagnosing the Physical

A wise counselor works in cooperation with medical science. Take, for example, Dr. Jack Morris, a Washington, D.C. area pastor who is a trained psychotherapist. Morris works closely with a team of medical doctors who are dedicated Christians, and the three of them work in harmony with each other. At times Morris will refer a client to the physician because he suspects that his emotional problem has physical roots. The physician, in turn, when a person has come for medical treatment but his problem is diagnosed as being more emotional or spiritual, will send the person to Morris, who can help the patient work out the conflict. That makes sense!

How do you know when a problem may have physical roots? Much of the time you quickly identify mood changes, depression, exhaustion, or boredom. The individual seems to be on good speaking terms with God. You can't really see a spiritual conflict; you can't see any root problems which are emotionally caused. The individual is not in conflict with anybody. He seems to like his job. He doesn't feel trapped in a hopeless situation, such as working for someone he doesn't like and not wanting to quit for fear of not getting another job. You can suppose that there may be a physical problem resulting in these mood shifts.

"How long has it been since you have had a complete physical?" I often ask, and the usual reply is, "I don't remember, but a long time."

"O.K., before we get together again, I want you to go see your doctor, and I especially want him to check your blood sugar."

Why? Your diet and your blood sugar affect your emotions and your moods. For example, hypoglycemia, low blood sugar, may produce lethargy and even depression. Or a husband's inability to function sexually may not be emotional; it may be the result of sugar diabetes which has been undiagnosed and untreated.

Telling people that God loves them and has a plan for their lives is good, but what they sometimes need is to realize part of that plan is to let the doctor show them the physical problems and how to deal with them.

On one occasion I counseled with a woman who began telling me how physically weary she was all of the time, how she had to lie down periodically when she was doing her housework. She explained there were times when she felt good and at other times she really was hurting. She had gone to her doctor, who told her nothing was wrong with her and suggested that she see a psychiatrist.

She wept bitter tears as she said, "Even my husband doesn't believe me when I tell him that I feel bad. He thinks that I'm faking it when I really hurt. Sometimes I think maybe I am going crazy!"

She wasn't crazy! She had *lupus erythematosus* (a skin disorder) which was eventually diagnosed by a specialist. When she learned what her problem was, it didn't disappear, but the emotional conflict of thinking something was wrong with her mind was gone, and doctors began to treat the underlying source of difficulty.

When you hurt physically, your spiritual life is also affected. The life of Elijah demonstrates forcibly that even spiritual giants get tired and discouraged and feel like quitting when they are exhausted physically. That's something we often forget.

The story of Elijah's confrontation with the four hundred fifty prophets of Baal is the stuff that missionaries like to put in their prayer letters. Tremendous victory! Fire from heaven falls and vindicates the lone prophet of God. Even Lee Iacocca, who turned Chrysler around, couldn't brag about one like that. It was definitely a win-win situation.

But the next morning Jezebel, the wife of King Ahab,

sent a messenger to Elijah, saying, "So let the gods do to me, and more also, if I do not make your life as the life of one of them by tomorrow about this time" (1 Kings 19:2). Suddenly, Elijah's sky turned gray, and the man of God turned and ran for his life. Is this the spiritual giant who prayed down fire from heaven and single-handedly withstood the hundreds of false prophets? A giant, or a gnat who flees?

Same man, all right, but one who was physically and emotionally exhausted. "Elijah was a man just like us," says James (5:17 NIV), and in that statement there is a tremendous insight. You aren't an iron man or an Amazonian woman! When you are physically exhausted, your emotional outlook and your relationship with God will be affected, which is why James instructed us to "pray for one another" (5:16). It happened to Elijah along with scores of other biblical greats, and you must understand what's happening when you are affected the same way.

Diagnosing the Spiritual

I was a young pastor of my first church when Sam Jones met me in my office. This big bear of a man thrust a roll of bills into my hand as he said, "Here, this is the money for the shock treatments I was supposed to have but that I no longer need!"

Sam had been in psychiatric treatment for several years without success. He would stay with one doctor for a while and when nothing happened, he would find another. The latest series of shock treatments hadn't helped him erase the memories of a troubled past. But when he received Jesus Christ as his Savior and came to understand that his past was forgiven, forgotten, and wiped away as though it had never taken place (see Ps. 103:12), his problem rapidly dissipated.

The psychiatrist recognized his rapid improvement and the shock treatments were canceled. It was one of my first encounters with the dynamic way in which Jesus Christ can totally change a person's emotional outlook.

It is no wonder that Dr. Paul DuBois, a psychotherapist, says, "Religious faith is the best preventative against the maladies of the soul, mind, and body, and is the most powerful medicine we have ever discovered for curing them." I agree!

Over the years I have seen scores of men and women with deeply troubled lives who completely changed through faith in Jesus Christ—alcoholics (some of whom had tried eighteen different cures), drug addicts, homosexuals, and moral, decent people whose lives were so bound by fear they couldn't step outside their homes.

Disciplines that fail to recognize the essential spiritual nature of mankind are bound to be impotent when it comes to treating the maladies of the spirit. When we have stepped outside of the will of God, we have a spiritual problem. The answer is to deal with what it really is—sin, and get back into harmony with the will of the Father.

Jonah, the prophet, has been reproduced in the lives of millions of men and women who went to church as children but "outgrew" their faith in their teen years or in college. They turned their backs on God and lived as though there were no God, no accountability, or no eternal hereafter.

Jonah's problem was spiritual! He was out of the will of God for his life. The result was (in his own words), "My soul fainted within me" (Jon. 2:7)—that was the spiritual problem. The physical one may have been high blood pressure which threatened to blow off the top of his head. Giving Jonah little white pills for blood pressure wasn't what he needed. Only repentance, confession, and striking out in a new direction could solve his problem.

Dealing gently but insistently with people as you help them gain God's perspective during *phase one*, opens the door for the person to evaluate the options in *phase two*, and then turn the corner spiritually in *phase three*, choosing the path of God's will.

Undiagnosed and ignored, spiritual afflictions result in a great deal of emotional suffering and even physical pain for people. The apostle Paul recognized this in the Corinthian church: ". . . many are weak and sick among you, and many sleep [are dead]" (1 Cor. 11:30).

Dr. Jack Kelly, one of Scotland's finest cardiologists, was once talking with me about the emotional and spiritual needs of people. He related how on one occasion, he had been asked to examine a patient who was suffering with "heart pains." He found no physical malady. Being a dedicated believer, however, he began to question his patient further, only to discover that the patient had recently returned from Paris and was suffering an acute case of guilt because of sexual misconduct. Although most cardiologists' skills run out when the electrocardiogram looks normal, Jack Kelly knew how to treat both problems.

The answer to spiritual guilt lies in applying the resources of forgiveness and cleansing through the blood of Jesus Christ, a solution which you can prescribe freely as a layman.

When Larry Crabb finished his doctoral program in clinical psychology, he had divided the problems of people into two categories: "emotional problems" and "spiritual problems." Speaking of that division Crabb says, "I regarded the resources of Christianity as welcome additions to the Christian therapist's little black bag of techniques. However, I distinguished clearly between *psychological* problems and *spiritual* problems. For solving psychological problems, I believed that Christianity was often helpful but rarely essential."[1]

However, as Crabb began to work with people, he discovered that people often came to him complaining of surface problems. But when he began to work with them, he couldn't put his finger on any substantial problem. He says, "Probing more deeply, I noticed that this person had a lot of foolish ideas about life that took no real account of God, and that he or she had a stubborn inclination to do wrong and an equally stubborn unwillingness to admit being wrong."[2]

At that point Crabb realized that he was dealing with problems which couldn't really be labeled as "mental disease" but rather "required far more than psychology could offer."

Instead of considering Christianity as something which was "helpful but not essential," Crabb began to see it as "essential in solving personal prolems," seeing a personal relationship with Christ as "a necessary foundation for dealing with all problems, psychological or spiritual."[3]

Guiding a person into the will of God means "deprogramming" a lot of the ideas which have permeated our society, such as:

- My fulfillment is the most important thing in the world.
- My happiness is imperative.

- Enough money would solve any problem.
- Someone else could probably better meet my needs.
- Sex may not be everything in life, but it's way ahead of whatever is in second place.
- If I were only more beautiful, I would be loved.
- If you really loved me, you would know what I think.

In a secular world believers are bombarded by philosophies and ideologies which run counter to God's plan and purpose for their lives. At the same time, our sinful nature constantly wars against God's plan for our lives.

If the person who came to you for help fully saw this and understood the implications of his past actions, he or she probably would not be faced with the present difficulties. Recognizing the cause, however, will help him arrive at a solution.

Another failure resulting in improper diagnosis is not hearing what the person you are helping is really saying. Your communication skills are important, and if they are lacking, you can develop them. Obviously, you can't be listening at the same time your mind is going ahead of what the person is saying. Neither can you listen very well if you are thinking about the responsibilities you carry and how you really ought to be doing something other than listening to the person who hurts.

Take time, listen, pray, and evaluate, and only then will you be ready to respond to the question, "What do you think I should do?"

I will talk about diagnosing the emotional aspects of a person in Chapter 8, which is devoted to counseling people with emotional problems from a biblical perspective. For now, let's examine the difference between counseling from a biblical perspective and counseling from a secular perspective.

6

Counseling "by the book" or by the Book?

(How Secular and Biblical Counseling Differ)

An experiment was conducted recently by psychologists at Vanderbilt University who wanted to know if the advice of untrained, nonprofessionals who were warm and cordial was as effective as that of trained psychotherapists. The group of professionals, some of the best in their area, had an average of twenty-three years experience behind them. The second group were college professors who had no formal experience or training in counseling.

Both groups worked with troubled people for no more than twenty-five hours, and at the end of that time comparisons were made. The results: "Patients undergoing psychotherapy with college professors showed . . . quantitatively as much improvement as patients treated by experienced professional psychotherapists."[1]

In an unrelated article the *Washington Post*'s magazine, *Insight*, decries the impotence of psychoanalysis saying, "Were surgeons to have the same cure rate as psychoanalysts, there would be no surgery; they would all be in prison on malpractice charges."[2]

It is only natural that the professionals view studies such as these with disdain. In the field of psychiatry there is probably less agreement among professionals as to what really works than there is in any other scientific discipline.

Psychiatrist Garth Wood, in his book *The Myth of Neurosis: Overcoming the Illness Excuse,* breaks with the traditions of his profession, arguing that nontrained professionals are some of the best sources of help for people.[3] He's convinced that you who have an intimate knowledge of another person can be a powerful force and catalyst for good in the life of a friend. After all, you know the strengths and weaknesses of your friend; you know the habit patterns, idiosyncrasies of personality, and what motivates that person. You start with an edge that the professional can gain only by hours of conversation and prodding.

For you who know Christ as your personal Lord and Savior, there is an additional source of wisdom and insight: the indwelling presence of the Holy Spirit. During Passion Week Jesus spoke of the coming Holy Spirit four times.[4] He used a term which had not previously been used for the Holy Spirit, *paraklatos,* a word which is translated as "counselor" in the Bible. Jesus told the disciples that He would ask the Father to send them another Counselor, who would guide them into truth and show them things to come. This is the same One who indwells the child of God today and can give him insights that he would never have otherwise.

Perhaps you are asking, "Do you really believe that?" I am convinced, on the basis of my own experience, that the Holy Spirit will help you focus on things that people say which lead to vital issues. "It just happens!" you say. I don't think so. God knows the future; He also knows the past in ways that you do not, and as you counsel, He will prompt you to ask questions and give you new insights that you would otherwise not have. The Holy Spirit serves as the Counselor who guides you and helps the person you counsel move into the will of God.

The Holy Spirit and Counseling

The Holy Spirit, the third person of the Trinity, is holy because holiness is part of the nature of God. Behind the word "holy" are two concepts: purity and separation. He is not an abstract or a philosophical idea, but a person with the will and the mind of God. He brings conviction. He guides us into truth. He is the agent of conversion; and when it comes to counseling, He is the source of lasting personality change as our old nature gives way to Christlikeness.

For centuries people have debated the issue of nature versus nurture—heredity versus environment, yet it matters little when the Holy Spirit begins to work in a life, a process which is described as "sanctification" in the New Testament. Three times we are told this work of "knocking off the rough edges" of our old nature is the work of God's Holy Spirit.[5]

In the first century, to call a person a "Corinthian" slurred that person's character and morality. People who lived in this ancient city didn't boast of their family heritage as did the Athenians. Crowning the acropolis overlooking Corinth was the grand temple of Aphrodite, the goddess of sexuality, whose one thousand priestesses were merely glorified prostitutes. Adulterers, homosexuals, transvestites, alcoholics, extortioners, and perverts were among those mentioned by

Paul in his letter to the Corinthians. Then following this list, Paul says, "And such were some of you. But you were . . . sanctified . . . by the Spirit of our God" (1 Cor. 6:11).

This grand work of sanctification by God's Holy Spirit in the lives of people is something that cannot be understood or duplicated in the secular world. It is the victory of the Spirit over both heredity and environment.

The Holy Spirit works through men and women who are in touch with Him—which means God uses *you* as you help people work through their problems. In his book *Competent to Counsel*, Jay Adams says, "The use of human agency in counseling . . . does not in itself bypass the work of the Spirit; to the contrary, it is the principal and ordinary means by which He works."[6]

In other words, God, through the agency of His Spirit, works in and through us to bring people into conformity with His will. You have an important part to play in restoring the order in the kingdom of God that was lost as the result of sin's dark entrance into the world. This is why you need to work in harmony with the Holy Spirit, and not against Him, in guiding people toward the will of God.

Why not use the Bible in conjunction with some of the modern techniques of psychology? Many techniques are amoral, neither good nor evil in themselves. We can learn something from these secular disciplines, but far too often, without realizing it, we adopt secular frameworks of counseling and baptize them with a sprinkling of Bible verses, and then we think we are counseling in a Christian context.

In his book *Psychological Seduction*, William Kirk Kilpatrick says:

True Christianity does not mix well with psychology. When you try to mix them, you often end up with a watered-down Christianity instead of a Christianized psychology. But the process is subtle and is rarely noticed. I wasn't aware that I was confusing two different things. And others in the church who might have been expected to put me right were under the same enchantment as I. It was not a frontal attack on Christianity—I'm sure I would have resisted that. It was not a case of a wolf at the door: the wolf was already in the fold, dressed in sheep's clothing. And from the way it was petted and fed by some of the shepherds, one would think it was the prize sheep.[7]

How Do People Get So Confused?

Often people find themselves in positions of leadership. They don't ask to be counselors; it just happens because they are Bible teachers, leaders of discussion groups, or outgoing persons to whom others are readily attracted. Others begin to look to them for guidance and help.

God blesses their efforts with modest success, but sometimes they struggle with inadequacies. They are like the counselor who thinks, "I could help people a lot more if I had some training." Uncertain of where or how to get that training, the individual may enroll in a secular psychology course at a local university.

I have known some men with Bible school or seminary training who took secular training in counseling and didn't even recognize that the methods which were taught violated scriptural principles. Others were overwhelmed by the secular assault on their faith.

Alex was like that. He grew up in the church, went to seminary, and then became a pastor who had a real heart for people. As the counseling load grew, he realized that he needed more tools. Feeling that he could better help people if he were a psychiatrist, Alex gave up his church, enrolled in medical school at University of California at Berkeley, and became a psychiatrist.

By the time he finished his work in psychiatry, Alex, to the great regret and confusion of his family and friends, gave up his faith. Today he no longer attends church or believes in God. "Anything you want to believe is fine if it works," he tells his clients.

For far too long we evangelicals have had an "intellectual inferiority complex" thinking that the secular world has a corner on knowledge that we don't have. "If we are really going to find acceptance in the world," we reason, "we had better take the best of what the gospel has and cloak it with the intellectualism that secular disciplines offer."

That complex is an old one. Remember that the children of Israel wanted a king "to be like other nations" (1 Sam. 8:20). "They have not rejected you," God told Samuel, "but they have rejected me" (1 Sam. 8:7). Their desire for a king resulted in bondage. Any time we desire something which is outside of the plan and purpose of God, we may get it but we pay the price of bondage to have it. It isn't that some non-Christian professors aren't intelligent; it's simply that they know so many things which are in violation of God's guidelines, and both cannot be true.

How Secular Counseling Models Differ from the Biblical Model

At the risk of oversimplification, I'd like to point out the fact that there are three basic secular models used in counseling today which differ rather dramatically from the biblical model I have presented. The moral model comes the closest to it, but still offers no absolutes; instead it holds a subjective concept of ethics which is different for different people.

	FREUDIAN MODEL	MEDICAL MODEL	MORAL MODEL	BIBLICAL MODEL
ROOT OF THE PROBLEM	Victim of Conscience or Environment	Victim of Chemistry; Mental illness (like a virus from without)	Violator of Morality (standards too high)	Violator of will of God
CURE	Psychoanalysis (6 to 8 yrs.)	Psychotherapy Drugs	Psycho-therapy (talking cures)	Confession Repentance Restoration Restitution

Another approach would be to contrast the major premises of secular disciplines with the biblical model.

SECULAR MODELS	BIBLICAL ALTERNATIVES
1. Follow the ground rules of the school's founder such as Freud, Mowrer, Adler, Jung, or whomever.	1. Follow the principles of Scripture.
2. Are man-centered or client-centered, thus God is unimportant.	2. Relate man to God and thus accept scriptural guidelines for interpersonal relations.
3. Struggle with lack of clearly defined areas of responsibility.	3. Man is responsible and can change. Recognizes sin and forgiveness.

4. Offer no lasting hope that life will be different.	4. Changed character promises the hope of a better future.
5. Often end in failure and may result in further despair and bondage.	5. Leads to change.

Have I been too hard on secular disciplines? I am not suggesting that all non-Christian counselors have nothing to offer, but I am saying that philosophical models that leave God out do not offer solutions which go to the heart of problems that have taken us outside the will of God.

Some men, who basically follow the moral model, have indeed helped many people and have, at times, stopped just short of what the Bible says about responsibility and grace. For example, Dr. Thomas Szasz, sometimes called the "anti-psychiatric psychiatrist," has for many years denounced the irresponsibility of psychoanalysis, which he considers to be an endless search to hang responsibility on something or someone else. And he is not alone. For at least twenty years before his death in 1983, O. Hobart Mowrer denounced the psychoanalytic theories of Freud. He called for increasing the power of conscience and spoke of "a very present hell on this earth, the hell to which unexpiated sin and guilt lead us."

More recently Garth Wood, the outspoken critic of psychiatry (who, don't forget, is himself a psychiatrist), alleges that far too much credence has been given to the idea that people suffer from a disease which we call "neurosis," just as people suffer from mumps or pneumonia. He contends that the medical model of mental illness (you are attacked by mental illness just as you would get a cold or the flu) has little, if any, validity. He says that neurosis is a myth. Wood believes that the cure comes through first admitting wrongdoing, and then through atonement, doing something which rectifies the wrong and leads to mental health. Yet Wood still stops short of biblical truth. Fuller Seminary professor H. Newton Malony, in reviewing his book, charges that Wood "seems far less interested in what is right than in what will work."[8]

The contrast between the mentality of the secular person and the individual in whom the Spirit of God dwells is nothing new. Paul experienced this struggle in Corinth as he tried to communicate the difference that a personal knowledge of Jesus Christ really makes. Almost as though he was giving up trying to relate to the secular mind, he says, "The natural man does not receive the things of the Spirit of God, for they are foolishness to him; nor can he know them, because they are spiritually discerned" (1 Cor. 2:14).

What difference does this Christian attitude make as we strive to help people?

Counseling in Cooperation with the Spirit of God

Biblical Counseling is God-centered

Most secular counseling is man-centered and deals with "felt needs." The temptation for the Christian who has been trained in a secular environment is to keep man at the center and bring God into his life in such a way that God becomes a spiritual "band-aid" to get man off the hook when he is in trouble.

The whole focus is wrong! We must understand there

will never be enough pieces to fit the puzzle of life's problems together apart from a relationship with God. This is why Jesus Christ came. God's plan is to bring us into harmony with His divine will and thus to change our natures through the new birth.

As long as thinking is fuzzy in this regard, we will never see the larger picture, and our image of God will only be a reflection of our own natures. Our God will be too small!

Biblical Counseling Recognizes the Sinfulness of Human Nature

This is not to imply that anyone who struggles with a problem is suffering from sin, but it does recognize that most of the problems that require counseling are the result of man's sinful nature. Notice the cataloging of the characteristics of the flesh or man's sinful nature recorded in Galatians 5:19–21, the very factors creating unhappiness today. Among the list are "adultery, fornication, uncleanness, licentiousness, idolatry, sorcery, hatred, contentions [arguments], jealousies, outbursts of wrath, selfish ambitions, dissensions, heresies, envy, murders, drunkenness, revelries, and the like."

When the Bible says, "For all have sinned and fall short of the glory of God," and "There is none righteous, no, not one," (Rom. 3:23,10), it becomes obvious that even the best of people bear the incipient dregs of rottenness which are found in the worst of people. And, inversely, in the worst of people there will still be certain qualities which reflect the fact that man was made in the image of the divine.

Have you ever had the experience of going to your garden to till the soil and finding a boulder or an old rotten board that had to be moved? As you picked it up, dozens, possibly hundreds of creeping, crawling bugs and slugs began to squirm. Such is what is dredged up from the recesses of the heart because of our old natures. Speaking of the heart as the seat of our affections and choices, Jeremiah wrote, "The heart is deceitful above all things, and desperately wicked; Who can know it?" (Jer. 17:9).

How else can you explain the humiliation and devastating consequences which have followed the poor choices some Christians make, choices which resulted in actions totally out of character with the lives those individuals had lived over the years? To their dying days they will regret the decisions which embodied the sordid thoughts within. Realizing that none of us is immune from the same, Paul warns, "Therefore let him who thinks he stands take heed lest he fall" (1 Cor. 10:12).

The nature of this book isn't theological, and I won't attempt an exhaustive treatment of sin, but in connection with this study, I need to point out that Isaiah 53:6 is a clear picture of what sin does to our relationship to the will of God. It leads us astray from the right path, and the end result is unhappiness.

Biblical counseling recognizes that a person, no matter who he is, sins because of the pull of his old sinful nature, as well as because of his personal choices, so that none may say, "I'm not responsible; I couldn't help it!" We sin by nature *and* by choice; the end result is problems which create situations that we just can't handle without outside help.

Though sin is a spiritual problem, the emotional natures of our lives, our relationships with each other, and how we feel about ourselves are affected. All of this is part of our mental image and health.

Discouragement and despair are the marks of the mentally ill, who have struggled with their problems month after month, in some cases year after year. To tell people that their behavior is perfectly normal, and that they must simply learn to accept it, is to sentence them to a life of perpetual despair.

Suppose you went to a dentist with a toothache, and he took a look at your abscessed gum and said, "Hmm, that tooth doesn't look very good, but, friend, there's nothing to worry about. Everybody here is troubled with this kind of problem. The great solution is acceptance and understanding."

If somebody told you that, you would get another dentist and fast!

To tell someone, "Look, your problem is sin! But there is an answer to this problem!" is neither cruel nor devastating. It defines the malady and offers a solution.

Notice how different are the approaches to the problems of people:

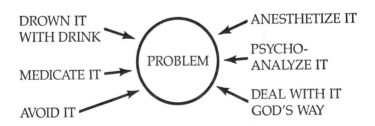

Counseling in the flesh masks sin as "sickness" which can be medicated, lived with, or removed. Your job as a counselor-friend is not that of a surgeon (removing the problem), but rather that of one who holds the flashlight so the person himself can see the problem. Then let God's Spirit do the surgery.

My son and I once backpacked high into the Sierras to enjoy the magnificent scenery and get away from civilization. While we were fishing in some of the high lakes, Steve somehow got a backlash in his fly line that sank the barbed hook deeply into his hand. Calmly he walked over and said, "Dad, I've got a problem."

"What is it?" And he showed me.

We walked back to camp considering the options we had. The first was to break camp, hike down, and find a doctor who could do the appropriate surgery to remove the hook.

Not much liking the idea of giving up the rest of the trip, we began to look for other options.

"What do we have that could help us get this thing out?" I wondered.

When I had exhausted my inventory of ideas, Steve asked, "Dad, do you have a new double-edged razor blade in your pack?"

I had one. I sterilized it; then with a steady hand Steve calmly performed minor surgery on himself and removed that unwanted fish hook! His was the right solution.

Your task as a biblical counselor isn't to say, "That's a dumb thing you did," (Who in their right mind would sink a fishing hook into their hand miles from civilization?) but to help find the solution.

In dealing with problems which have taken people outside the will of God, you don't have to berate or condemn them, but help them identify the problem and correct it by following the next guideline.

*Biblical Counseling Follows the Principles
of God's Word, the Bible*

Many of the situations which cause people to reach
out to others for guidance are situations which merely
necessitate decisions of one kind or another. We live in a
world of stress, and at times we need someone to say,
"Look, you are on the right track; keep moving," reinforcing what the person feels is the will of God for his or
her life.

At times we assume work loads and burdens which
exceed our capacity to handle them. Sometimes I illustrate this truth by pointing to the podium or the table
which holds my speaking notes and asking, "How
many of you think I could stand on this table?"

Those who are still awake raise their hands.

Then I ask, "If I stand on this and have a couple more
people stand on it, how many think it will support us?"

Obviously, the stress increases in direct proportion to
the weight on the top, and at some point it will collapse.

Another illustration I often use is that of fish swimming in a pond. When a fisherman comes along and
hooks one of the fish and begins to pull, the fish begins
to swim erratically, flopping back and forth in the water
as the pressure is exerted by the fisherman. Other fish
swimming in the pond think, "He really looks crazy;
look at all the funny gyrations our brother fish is going
through." The more pressure some of us face, the
greater our need for someone to relieve the pressure
causing our erratic behavior. That's why you become
important as a counselor.

Dr. Karl Menninger used to illustrate sanity and in-
sanity as being on two opposite ends of a line forming a
continuum such as this:

SANITY	INSANITY

ABILITY TO FUNCTION	INABILITY TO FUNCTION

Menninger contended that everyone moves back and forth on this continuum. On some days you feel completely in control; on other days you feel driven and pushed by your schedule, at the mercy of your emotions and you don't like it. When you reach the point where you are no longer able to function, you need help.

The Bible offers sound counsel when it comes to the issues of life. I am convinced that one of the greatest needs of people today is to understand what the Bible says about handling the problems causing what we describe as mental illness.

Few people who fill the pews of churches today understand what it really means to be forgiven, to be adopted as a child of God, and brought into the family of God. Having never been confronted with the sovereignty of God, they are overly concerned with the multitude of worries which drive them into the asphalt. Not understanding the will of God, they struggle, often against Him, in trying to put things together which are not really in their best interests.

Vast resources in the Bible can be brought to bear on our personal needs (see Chapters 7, 8, and 9 for specific Scriptures that deal with problems such as worry and fear). The greater our knowledge of God's plan for our lives, the less will be the need for individual counseling.

One of the greatest services a pastor can do for the

mental health of his people is not necessarily to spend long hours in counseling (which is important), but to faithfully teach and proclaim the Word. As he does that, he will discover that most of the people who need counseling are coming from *outside* his church. They will not be the people who sit in his congregation Sunday after Sunday.

You who are involved in study groups, whether you are a teacher, a discussion leader, or set up chairs for the meeting, are on the front lines of building solid lives and contributing to good mental health. You're doing preventative therapy!

Biblical Counseling Results in Liberation, Not in Further Bondage

There is no frustration as great as that suffered by a person who has gone from psychiatrist to psychiatrist, hoping for help but always being told that nothing can be done. To describe a person's problem as a "sickness" which can only be medicated or, at best, suppressed, offers no hope that life can be different.

Such was the despair of William, who had been under the care of a psychiatrist for nineteen years. "How did you hear about me?" I questioned when my phone rang and William asked if he could see me. A friend had told him that I could help, and as I sat down that first afternoon and listened to him and his wife pour out their hearts, I sensed that the greatest need in their lives was for a personal relationship with Jesus Christ. Though I seldom share the plan of salvation on anyone's first visit, I opened my Bible and explained how great God's love toward us is in sending His Son to be our Savior, and that when we receive Him as Lord and Master, we become new persons in Christ Jesus.

When William returned the following week, he reported that he had never been so happy as he had been that week. Part of his difficulty was an unresolved problem of guilt which could never be tranquilized completely. I began working with William, applying biblical principles to the needs of his life.

Step number two was to get William to a doctor who would begin to decrease the daily dosage of tranquilizers and supervise an exercise program. I remember when I met William for a morning walk that first week that he seemed to plod with one foot barely getting in front of the other. But as the decrease in tranquilizers began to let his body's natural energy take over, it was only a matter of weeks until he was completely free of drugs and was a new man with a new marriage.

"For to be carnally minded is death, but to be spiritually minded is life and peace" (Rom. 8:6). God's principles really work.

7

*Using the Bible in Counseling
Relational Problems*

The next three chapters will help you use the Bible in dealing with problems involving relationships, problems of the emotions, and problems relating to addictive behavior. I do not intend for them to be in-depth studies, but rather guides which can be applied to a wide spectrum of issues.

Many of the problems which will bring people to you are the results of their having missed the plan of God. A person traveling from San Francisco to New York may have successfully traversed the highways for two thousand miles (like a person with twenty-five good years of marriage), yet if he takes a wrong turn in Chicago (perhaps betraying his spouse), he may eventually end up in Toronto (or with a broken home). Having taken wrong turns, having made poor choices, at times having sinned, we have to readjust our paths and take new directions.

Everything that happens within the confines of a home affects all the members of that family because a family is an intricate pattern of relationships. It can only follow that much of our counseling involves relationships with people, especially those in our families. In a family of four there are at least sixteen separate relationships, the relationship of each person to the other three as well as an individual relationship (how we feel about ourselves) which affects our emotional health and happiness. No wonder family living is complex.

Illnesses, career reversals, accidents, financial problems, the birth or death of a child, even aging which changes our appearance and outlook are part of the tapestry of relationships. These generally have nothing to do with personal failure, nor are they the result of individual sin; nonetheless, they are issues which often require counseling and help to cope with.

What I've discovered as the result of reading the letters of the thousands of men and women who listen to our *Guidelines* radio and TV programs and who write for personal help is that we can never assume that individuals who are believers in Jesus Christ, and even involved in church, really have a very deep knowledge of Scripture.

Translated into the coffee cup counseling environment, this means you can't take anything for granted; you have to use the Word, showing people what God's perspective is and how it differs from ours. The application of God's Word, though, is a very positive thing which gives hope in a broken world. It takes away the despair of those who see no way out of their situation. It allows a broken person to see light at the end of a dark tunnel.

At times the people you help will have grown up in homes where a knowledge of right and wrong is clear. They may not always do the right thing, but at least they know what it is. A growing number of people, though, especially those under age forty, have been raised by permissive parents and have very fuzzy ideas about right and wrong.

Our role models and heroes today are often individuals whose integrity is tainted. They seem to be admired more because of what they do or get away with rather than what they are. "Integrity," says Ted Engstrom in his book by the same title, "simply put . . . is doing what you said you would do."[1] When it comes to marriage, it includes a monogamous commitment. In the family, integrity includes loyalty and trustworthiness. In friendships, it means support and acceptance.

When people don't do what they said they would do, or what the other person thinks they said they would do, conflict results and relationships are broken.

In Chapter 4, I said one of the goals of counseling is to get the individual you are helping to see himself as he or she really is. Another goal is to help the person see the situation from a mate's viewpoint (or the viewpoint of the person with whom there is conflict). A third goal, and most important of all, is for the person to see the issue from God's perspective, which then gives reason to initiate changes resulting in forgiveness and the restoring of broken relationships.

How you use the Word in doing this is critical. At times broken relationships are the result of unkept promises. At times they are the result of wrong choices which damage relationships, and, at other times, they are the result of misunderstandings or different points of view, which have to be reconciled through better communication and understanding.

In this book I haven't discussed the importance of clear communication at length, but it's vital in resolving broken relationships. Every time a person makes a statement there are three components:

1) What you said (the face value of the statement).

2) What you meant to say (which may not be what you actually said), and

3) What you implied (which you may not have actually said at all).

When we were living in Manila, Philippines, I took my twelve-year-old son to the exotic bird farm to take pictures of the rare and unusual birds. Both of us were photographing the birds as a peacock began to spread his tail feathers. I reached for my camera preparing to take a picture and said, "Get one!" meaning, "Get a picture of the bird."

But Steve immediately lunged for the tail feathers of the bird intending to pull one out. "No, Steve!" I yelled, "That's not what I meant."

"But, Dad, you said, 'Get one!'"

"Yes, but I meant 'Get a picture!'"

Here's how that translated:

1) I said, "Get one."
2) I meant, "Get a picture."
3) I implied, "Get a tail feather."

Communication broke down!

Jesus said, "Therefore, whatever you want men to do to you, do also to them . . ." (Matt. 7:12). This requires maintaining a keen awareness of how our actions affect other people. Working through conflict situations demands this.

John was on a business trip, and while he was away Mary spent hours on the phone talking to travel agents, airline reservation clerks, waiting, taking notes, getting the best deal for their summer vacation.

Wanting to clear the plans with her husband before she ordered non-refundable, no-change tickets, Mary called his office and left a message for him to return her call after dinner. But John didn't get the message.

An errant secretary finally remembered the next morning and interrupted a business meeting with the message to call home immediately.

John did and became angry and brusque because he had been called out of a meeting to hear about next summer's vacation. And Mary, who had no intention of interrupting a business meeting, felt that he was angry with her without cause. She was miffed that he cared so little about her hard work.

John didn't know that Mary had called the previous day. Mary didn't realize John was interrupted in a business meeting. Reconstructing the actual situation, both realized that they were blaming the other for something neither had control over. Clear communication and understanding helped them resolve the issue.

A Framework for Biblical Counseling

The following points are matters which you as a counselor need to resolve firmly in your thinking before you even begin to help others work through personal problems.

God Is a Good God; Therefore, What He Tells Us in His Word Is His Plan For Living

Of course, this cuts across the grain of secular images of God as a bully, or a cosmic policeman, out to get you when you are bad. Or the Great Enforcer whose black book (the Bible) was designed to make you miserable and is totally unrealistic and out of harmony with our world today.

Another version of this is that the Bible may be well and good, but it is only a lofty guide or something to shoot for, the "impossible dream" of old men with long gray beards who wrote it long ago.

When you counsel in a biblical perspective, you use the Bible to enlighten, to guide, and to encourage as well as to reprove and censure (when necessary).

Healing Broken Relationships Instead of Dissolving Them Is Working in Harmony with God's Plan

God could not be a good God realizing that there will be conflicts in relationships *unless* He had given us a means of resolving those conflicts.

The conflicts which destroy relationships today are not new. Infidelity, broken communication producing hostility and anger, premarital sex, jealousy, dishonesty, and deceit—all of these are pictured in the lives of those whose stories are told in the Bible.

Those who think there should be no conflicts in our relationships are about as realistic as expecting all Christian wives to be a combination of Betty Crocker, Mother Teresa, and Farrah Fawcett, and expecting every man to walk on water and leap over tall buildings in a single bound.

When two people come together in marriage, they "become one flesh," in the words of Scripture, but their union in marriage doesn't for a moment mean the bonding of their emotions or personalities. Every person is a collage of customs, emotions, family traditions, idiosyncrasies, and personalities; there is also the baggage of heredity which links you to your ancestors. The "becoming one" is the weaving of all these different ingredients into the tapestry of a new relationship forming the structure of a new family.

It is not without elements of struggle which affects relationships. Helping to resolve these conflicts is all part of the healing ministry of Christ.

Some Conflicts Are Not the Result of Personal Failure But Are the Result of Living in a Broken World

Today there is a widespread belief which just won't go away: "If what happens to me is good, it's obvious that God is blessing me; and if it's bad, it's the judgment of God or the devil who did it."

"Why was my baby born with five holes in her heart? Is God punishing her for what I did?" Those were the questions of a young mother I had just met. Before I could say anything, Susan began to unload the pent-up emotions of her heart. She grew up in a home where parents were strict disciplinarians. When she became a teenager she rebelled and sowed her share of wild oats in defiance of her parents' stern admonitions, "God's going to punish you for what you are doing!"

Then one day shortly after she married, she was walking down the street and heard music drifting through the open windows of a church. She stopped to listen and finally entered. That day Susan gave her heart to the Lord and became a Christian. Nonetheless, those words kept hammering her conscience, "God's going to get you for what you've done!"

A series of calamities befell the young couple, none of which were the judgment of God or the result of satanic attack. A flood destroyed their apartment, and they lost the wedding gifts friends had given to them.

Their first child was still-born, and now a little baby, not expected to live beyond age two, had been born with five tiny holes in her heart.

An imperfect world means that we are confronted with brokenness for which, at times, we bear no direct responsibility.

People will ask, "Why did God let this happen to me? Why did He fail me?" and you will have to answer, "God did not fail you—your husband failed you," or "your wife failed you!"

At times even searching for an answer is futile, yet a person tells something of his belief in God by the questions he asks of God. You can go crazy trying to come up with adequate explanations for situations. It is much better to help the hurting person realize God will meet us at the point of our deepest needs.

Consider, for example, the woman whose husband is forced to take a job overseas. She suspects that he is unfaithful to her, yet she desperately needs the income he provides to care for her seven children. Or consider the plight of an aged widow whose support comes from a son stricken with an incurable disease, or the husband who struggles with guilt because he allowed doctors to perform surgery which resulted in his wife's death. What of the wife who has forgiven her husband for his affair, yet has to cope with diminished income because he must also support the child which was born of infidelity?

Learning to cope with situations we cannot alter is part of the healing process, and some situations—the result of living in a broken world—cannot be resolved. To bear anger or bitterness toward another, or even toward God, is part of what destroys lives. Through counseling you help your friend to forgive those who have hurt him or her and to understand it was not God who failed. You help him or her to see God as a stronghold in times of trouble (see Nah. 1:7), and a hiding place in times of distress (see Pss. 32:7; 61:2). In so doing we learn to cope with what cannot be changed.

*God Promised to Be with Us in Times of Difficulty,
Not to Exempt Us from Them*

When a problem confronts a couple, one of two things will happen: the problem will either drive the two closer to the Lord and each other, or the problem will cause division and bitterness.

> Isaiah 43:2–3: When you pass through the waters, I will be with you; And through the rivers, they shall not overflow you. When you walk through the fire, you shall not be burned, Nor shall the flame scorch you. For I am the Lord your God, The Holy One of Israel, your Savior. . . .
> Nahum 1:7: The Lord is good, A stronghold in the day of trouble; And He knows those who trust in Him.
> Ephesians 1:11: In [Him] also we have obtained an inheritance, being predestined according to the purpose of Him who works all things according to the counsel of His will.
> Romans 8:28: And we know that all things work together for good to those who love God, to those who are the called according to His purpose.

When Susan asked the question about her little baby struggling for life in Children's Hospital, I knew that a trite answer would never satisfy her. We walked out into the hallway and talked. Tears coursed down her cheeks, and I listened. Realizing that I needed to hear all the story (Proverbs 18:13 says, "He who answers a matter before he hears it, It is folly and shame to him."), I arranged a series of counseling sessions.

Susan eventually understood that the baby's problem was not God's punishment of her sin in the life of this innocent child, nor was it the devil who in particular had singled her out to inflict his cruelty. She also had to come to new understanding of who God is.

The Issue of Forgiveness

In the process of helping Susan, I had to help her learn what it means to seek and find the forgiveness of God, why she needed to forgive her parents for the suffering she had endured because of their attitudes, and finally she had to learn to forgive herself as well for what she did in her teenage years before she became a Christian. Let's deal with those three major issues.

What Does God's Forgiveness Mean and Why Seek It?

Almost always when there is a broken relationship with another person, an individual's relationship with God is affected. Harsh words produce bitterness, and anger produces sin. In dealing with the needs of people, great healing comes in recognizing, confessing, and forsaking that sin.

When people pray with you, they begin to vent their emotions and a tremendous catharsis takes place. Tears replace anger, and the brokenness which results helps to restore fractured relationships. Finding God's forgiveness is part of phase three: the restoration phase of counseling.

Key Scriptures

1 John 1:9: If we confess our sins, He is faithful and just to forgive us our sins and to cleanse us from all unrighteousness.

Psalm 103:12,13: As far as the east is from the west, So far has He removed our transgressions from us. As a father pities his children, So the Lord pities those who fear Him.

Isaiah 43:25: "I, even I, am He who blots out your transgressions for My own sake; And I will not remember your sins."

Micah 7:19: You will cast all our sins Into the depths of the sea.

When people have hurt others, especially when children are involved, they often feel that they are beyond God's forgiveness.

Insights

You could point out that Moses killed a man prior to God's calling (see Exod. 2:11–13). Rahab, the prostitute who befriended the spies sent out by Joshua to investigate the land of Palestine, was grafted into the lineage of Christ (see Matt. 1:5). David known as a man after God's heart, was an adulterer and a party to murder (see 2 Sam. 11). Even the apostle Paul had a stained background prior to his conversion, for he caused the persecution and death of many Christians. God forgave all of them and changed their lives just as He will forgive the friend you are counseling.

No individual is beyond the hand of God to bring forgiveness and healing to his troubled heart and life. In helping people understand, I often quote Psalm 103:12, which says that our sins are as far as the east from the west, and then ask, "How far is the east from the west?" After thinking for a minute, people usually remember that the east and the west never meet. Had the psalmist said the north from the south (the north and south poles are some 12,420 miles apart), our sins would have been a measurable distance.

Again, Isaiah 44:22 mentions their sins being blotted out as something which God will never remember against us.

"You mean I'll never have to give an account for the abortion I once had?" a young woman asked when I shared that Scripture with her.

"Never again!" I replied.

God's forgiveness, which was the result of Jesus' shedding His blood and dying in our stead, means we are forgiven, brought into the family of God, and are the recipients of eternal life (see John 6:47). Because He has forgiven us, we must take the next step.

Forgiving Each Other

Broken relationships mean broken people, and through forgiveness we find the grace of God which mends and heals.

Like the scalpel in the hand of a surgeon which can bring healing or harm, confrontation can have positive or negative effects on a fragile relationship. It can be a very positive healing force by observing the following:

Choose the Time, Place, and Manner of Confrontation

This gives you time to release your anger and pray about the encounter. It gives you time to think through what you want to say and don't want to say. There are times when you need to get a handle on your emotions before you deal with issues. It's O.K. to say, "John, I'd like to talk with you about . . . after dinner this evening. It will give me time to get a handle on my feelings so I can say what I'm thinking and not say the wrong thing."[2]

Deal with the Issue; Don't Attack the Person with Whom There Is a Broken Relationship

Saying, "Your brother is a no-good bum!" will make sparks fly. After all, your wife was related to the brother—who came to visit and has stayed three months, eating your food, drinking your cokes, munching potato chips in your easy chair in front of your TV—long before she became your wife. But saying, "What can we do to help your brother find a job?" focuses on the problem of unemployment, not his personal habits.

Express Feelings in a Nonthreatening Way

Saying, "I feel that . . ." is better than saying, "You . . . (did such-and-such)." When you say, "I have a problem and I need your help," the person whom you are confronting stops being a combatant and becomes part of the problem-solving process.

Learn to Negotiate

Another term is "compromise," but that word has a connotation we try to avoid. Life is a matter of give and take (not "I give and you take"), and a harsh, unbending attitude does not resolve conflicts. Such a person may win the battle and lose the war.

Forgiveness means you surrender your right to hurt someone because they hurt you. It means that you extend the right to be wrong to someone else because God has done that very thing for you.

Susan hadn't wronged her parents. Actually, it was their harsh discipline and improper understanding of how God deals with us ("God's going to get you when you are bad!") that had crippled her emotionally. However, her attitude toward them was wrong. Eventually, she came to understand that her reaction to the wrong done to her by her parents was as wrong in a different way as the injustice which she sustained.

Key Scriptures

Matthew 6:14,15: "For if you forgive men their trespasses, your heavenly Father will also forgive you. But if you do not forgive men their trespasses, neither will your Father forgive your trespasses."
Luke 17:3: "Take heed to yourselves. If your brother sins against you, rebuke him; and if he repents, forgive him."
Ephesians 4:32: "And be kind to one another, tenderhearted, forgiving one another, just as God in Christ also forgave you."
Matthew 18:15: "Moreover if your brother sins against you, go and tell him his fault between you and him alone. If he hears you, you have gained your brother."

Insights
Most of us want to avoid the confrontation necessary to go to someone and say, "I'm sorry; forgive me." Yet Jesus said that is exactly what we need to do, and your part as a counselor-friend is to provide the support and encouragement to help someone do this.

Forgiving Yourself

It is often easier to seek and find the forgiveness of God than to forgive ourselves for what we have done, especially when we feel our mistakes have been visited on our children. In some cases our failures do affect our children, to say nothing of the harm we inflict on our mates. Yet when we have genuinely repented and found God's forgiveness, and sought and received the forgiveness of the one we have hurt, we have no alternative but to forgive ourselves as well.

Working through this with Susan took a period of weeks. Two passages helped her: Romans 8:14–17 and Galatians 4:4–6. Both of them talk about God sending forth His Spirit into our hearts at conversion, adopting us into His family. The word used in the New Testament for adoption was a legal word which literally meant "the placing of a son."

A picture of human adoption illustrates this great truth. An infant, rejected by his or her birth parents or orphaned by circumstances no one could control, is accepted and loved by someone else.

In biblical days when an individual was adopted by someone, he went before a judge and a legal transaction took place. He received a new name and a new family. The past was forever obliterated even to the extent that if a person had committed crimes, he or she could never be held responsible for them. The old person ceased to exist in the sight of the law; a new one came into being.

When broken relationships are restored, emotions are affected, which leads to the next major subject: using the Bible to help with emotional problems.

But there's one more thing about Susan's baby that you will want to know. That little baby with five tiny holes in her heart, then only a few days old, didn't die by age two as the doctors had predicted. Amazingly, the holes in her heart knit on their own—something doctors didn't understand, but it happened. Susan and I have some idea why. As I counseled with her, I prayed, "Oh God, let that child live so that this mother will know when you forgive us, you wipe the slate clean as though we had never sinned. Help her to understand that you don't punish our children for sins which you have forgiven."

At my last contact with Susan, the baby had become a very normal teenager.

8

*Using the Bible in
Counseling Emotional Problems*

Time and space do not allow me to deal completely with the subject of how you help people who are struggling with emotional problems. We'll apply scriptural principles to four major emotions interwoven with many of the problems that bring people to you as a counselor-friend: anger, fear, worry, and depression.

Emotions are to life what pigment is to paint: they make life bright and beautiful or dark and dreary. Indeed, life would be mechanical and lacking intensity without emotions. But when emotions become damaged, just as a river which overflows its banks creates destruction, something beautiful becomes ugly. When a person becomes overwhelmed by his emotions, his family, friends, and acquaintances suffer too. But far more than the suffering which the person causes is the internal turmoil and intensity which he or she must face, often alone and misunderstood.

There is an issue, though, which needs to be confronted as we begin this chapter. Does God really want His children to suffer emotionally?

Is God pleased when we are overwhelmed with worry or fear? Is He pleased when two who once loved each other are continually torn by emotional conflict? Is there anything that glorifies Him about individuals who were once productive but have become stressed to the point of emotional "burnout"?

My question is not whether we ought to face emotional conflict, but rather is He pleased by our succumbing to it? In the upper room shortly before Jesus faced Calvary, He told the disciples, "In the world you will have tribulation; but be of good cheer, I have overcome the world" (John 16:33). The word translated "tribulation" is a word which is also translated in the New Testament as oppression, affliction, or difficult circumstances.[1] All of this spells emotional pressure, or stress, as we often refer to it today.

Paul, of course, saw more than his fair share of emotional conflict. His commitment to Jesus Christ and his determination to make Christ known created conflict as does our faith today in some situations. In today's society a woman who is a committed believer will experience similar conflict with her unbelieving husband about her spending time with a Bible study group or about her giving money to her church.

The letter which we know as 2 Corinthians has been called the "heart of Paul." In this magnificent letter, Paul laid aside doctrinal concerns which had occupied much of his previous letter and quite intimately shared his heart with these struggling people, so immature in their own Christian experiences. Possibly, Paul wanted them to know that even he struggled with emotional issues and conflicts, but he also wanted them to know that the struggle isn't the important thing—the victory is. He wrote, "Thanks be to God who always leads us in triumph in Christ" (2 Cor. 2:14).

Ponder these words for a moment:

From the Jews five times I received forty stripes minus one. Three times I was beaten with rods; once I was stoned; three times I was shipwrecked; a night and a day I have been in the deep; in journeys often, in perils of waters, in perils of robbers, in perils of my own countrymen, in perils of the Gentiles, in perils in the city, in perils in the wilderness, in perils in the sea, in perils among false brethren; in weariness and toil, in sleeplessness often, in hunger and thirst, in fastings often, in cold and nakedness—besides the other things, what comes upon me daily: my deep concern for all the churches (2 Cor. 11:24–28).

In the same letter he said he was "sorrowful, yet always rejoicing; as poor, yet making many rich; as having nothing, and yet possessing all things" (2 Cor. 6:10).

What a contrast of emotions! Whatever we face, Paul probably experienced too. Shortly before his death, the tough old warrior wrote to a young man from prison saying, "God has not given us a spirit of fear, but of power and of love and of a sound mind" (2 Tim. 1:7).

That sound-mind principle which Paul spoke of is possible because of these things: a relationship with Jesus Christ deals with the fundamental issue of guilt and forgiveness; the Bible teaches us how to handle the disappointments and hardships of life which are very much part of the broken world in which we live; and faith eliminates the ultimate fear of death, which allows us to focus on living vibrant, meaningful, and purposeful lives.

Paul's letters echo what he experienced in life: in the world we will face trouble and pressure, but through faith in God we can overcome the emotional conflicts and pressures that are fatal to many.

Once in San Diego a hot-air balloon was being filled preparatory to its flight. But in the process, the balloon pulled loose from its anchorage. Some of the people holding the ropes which had anchored the balloon immediately turned loose. Others held on tightly, thinking they could hold the balloon steady; but as the balloon slowly lifted from the ground, they could no longer hang on and plunged to their deaths below. A few, however, seeing what was happening, pulled themselves up the rope, hand over hand, and making a loop in the rope, rode with the balloon as it lazily rose in the air.

What Paul chose to do was to refuse to give up when confronted with emotional issues that would have caused lesser individuals to "turn loose" and give up. "I know how to be abased, and I know how to abound. . . . I have learned both to be full and to be hungry, both to abound and to suffer need," and then he wrote, "I can do all things through Christ who strengthens me" (Phil. 4:12,13).

"Yeah, I know," you may be thinking. "But I'm not one of those supermen who can climb the rope and ride it out." The point of Paul's life and teachings is that the circumstances of life cannot dictate our emotional and spiritual responses. We either become overcomers or are overcome by the circumstances.

When someone comes to you for help and you sense that the person's mind is poisoned with hatred and anger, you understand from the beginning that you are working with a situation which is contrary to God's will. You realize that you are working in cooperation with the Spirit of God to help that person forsake the anger and restore a relationship.

When you see a mother overwhelmed by irrational

fear which keeps her captive within her own home and so destroys her peace of mind that she cannot back the family car down the driveway and take her children to school, you are dealing with a situation which is not God's will (remember 2 Tim. 1:7 quoted earlier in this chapter?).

When you talk with a business colleague who has made some poor investments and is so worried about the money that he can't sleep nights and lives on a diet of double-strength Maalox and crackers, you know you are working with someone who needs the peace that comes through viewing life from the perspective of what really counts.

Christian faith becomes the framework of our emotional outlook, which is different from the secular mind, as Paul wrote, "Let this mind be in you which was also in Christ Jesus" (Phil. 2:5). Dr. Chris Thurman of the Minirth-Meier Clinic has written an excellent book, *The Lies We Believe,* to help people understand the secular lies that they accept as truth.

Once a person understands life from God's perspective, he or she will not be embittered by difficult situations.

Scott Bailey, one of our volunteers at Guidelines, was injured in a sports accident when he was a teenager and spent twenty-nine days in a coma. His recovery was marked by long years of physical therapy and trips to specialists of various kinds.

In spite of the physical handicap, which Scott will live with for the rest of his life, his outlook is bright, upbeat, and reflects the faith he has in his heart. When Scott was chided by an acquaintance who accused him of making his faith "a crutch," Scott replied, "Crutch, nothing! Jesus Christ has been my whole hospital!"

Let's examine some of the emotional issues which you have to deal with in helping people.

Uncontrollable Anger

Already in this book we've discussed several issues which involve anger: the husband who struck his wife when she didn't like the kitchen he was remodeling; the young mother who was angry with God for allowing her baby to be born with a defective heart; the wife who was angry and hurt because of her husband's affair.

Undoubtedly you will encounter people whose anger is out of control. The wife who has been betrayed by her husband is understandably angry, something different from the husband whose temper causes him to strike his wife or children. One is the result of confidence which has been betrayed; the other occurs because the man's emotions are out of control.

Insights

Anger in itself is not sin. It is amoral; it can either be used for good or misused, causing a great deal of heartache.

In the King James Version of the Bible the word *"anger"* occurs 234 times in 228 verses; the word *"angry"* 44 times in 43 verses. Many of those situations refer to God's anger because of the sins of His people. Jesus was angry with the Pharisees because of their unbelief (see Mark 3:5). Obviously, he was angry when he took a whip and drove the money changers from the temple. There is a time and a place for anger, but manifested in the wrong place, at the wrong time, and in the wrong manner, it becomes sin. That is why Paul urged the

Ephesians to "Be angry, and do not sin" (Eph. 4:26). You will have to help people work through misused or misdirected anger.

Paul recognized that wrath (strong anger) often works against us, provoking us to do things we later regret (see 1 Thess. 5:9 and 1 Tim. 2:8). James 1:19 says we are to be "slow to wrath." Following the passage where Paul urges us to be angry without sin, he says, "Do not let the sun go down on your wrath" (Eph. 4:26).

You can help people work through uncontrollable or harmful anger if you:

- Determine the cause (if possible) of anger and see if anything can be done to remove its source. This solution may require changes in lifestyle or even environment so that people who cause the anger are no longer encountered.
- If the source of anger can't be removed, encourage your friend to evaluate whether its cause is worth the emotional energy he is spending on it. Vance Havner used to say, "Any bulldog can whip a skunk, but sometimes it just ain't worth it!"
- Help your friend find appropriate ways of communicating feelings of anger without saying or doing things that would harm others.
- Suggest ways to relieve the stress which leads to angry outbursts. Physical recreation, hobbies, or leisure activities can serve as safety valves to vent emotional pressure.
- Help your friend realize that the indwelling presence of the Holy Spirit can tame that temper. Prayer is a means of accomplishing this as the angry person asks God to take control.

Key Scriptures

Ephesians 4:26 (quoted above) provides leverage for change. Ask him or her to memorize it with you. In the margin of your Bible at Ephesians 4:26, make a note of James 1:19, which gives motivation in dealing with this issue.

Irrational Fears

Insights

Fear of danger motivates a person to take steps to insure his safety; continual debilitating, enervating fear which shackles and robs him or her of peace of mind is not of God and must be overcome. Remember that telling someone how foolish it is to be afraid only intimidates a person and makes the problem worse.

Key Scripture

"For God has not given us a spirit of fear, but of power and of love and of a sound mind" (2 Tim. 1:7).

Most of our fears center around what has not happened but what we fear may happen, and what we do not understand. Men tend to fear things which threaten their male image, such as the loss of employment or the respect of their contemporaries. Women fear the loss of their physical beauty and whatever would rob them of their security.

Your friend Joy misses Bible study for several weeks, and you drop by to see her. As you sit down for a cup of tea together, you let her know that she has been missed. At first she talks about the babysitter who couldn't take care of the children, but then she bursts into tears and says, "Oh, I might as well tell you what's really bothering me. I don't know what's gotten into me, but lately whenever I start to back out the car, my hands get cold and sweaty and my heart beats like crazy. I'm scared to death that I'm going to get hit by another car. I don't know what's the matter with me. Dean says I must be losing my mind. Do you think I'm crazy?"

And you answer, "No, of course not; but do you think that there may be some connection between your feelings and the automobile accident you had last year?"

"I've thought about that. I don't know."

Ridicule or criticism won't work; instead encourage Joy to take the first step by driving to the post office a block away, or to take the kids to the school a mile away. Perhaps you care enough to go with her the first few trips. Or she may need to accept the reality of her fear of driving and then learn to take the bus or find a ride with another person.

Shortly after Darlene and I married, I learned that she had acrophobia (fear of heights). We had taken the elevator up the Eiffel Tower in Paris and to save a little money, we decided to walk down. We had gone only a short way down the stairs through the tower's exterior when she froze, and I discovered that heights really frighten her.

Three years ago, as we were skiing, she stopped on a slope, petrified of coming down. I had skied a few hundred yards farther and kept waiting for her to come too. About that time a ski patrol on a skimobile came by. I stopped him and asked him to go up and give her a ride down.

"Honey, it's O.K., you don't have to ski. It's all right," I told her. Instead of downhill skiing, we've become avid cross-country skiers, something she enjoys too.

Understanding that nothing outside God's will can happen to the child of God who is living and walking according to His purposes removes the feeling of being victimized by circumstances. Jack Morris, the psychotherapist I mentioned earlier, uses Psalm 23 with patients who are struggling with fear, asking them to memorize the psalm and quote it audibly several times a day. "Yea, though I walk through the valley of the shadow of death, I will fear no evil; For You are with me" (v. 4).

You can help people to cope with circumstances which could otherwise produce devastating fear. Understanding that safety is not "the absence of danger" but "the promise of the Lord's protection," they can live above fear which would otherwise destroy their peace of mind.

Pervasive Worry

Insights

No matter how many of us indulge in the practice, worry is sin. No individual can worry and trust God at the same time; you have to help your friend see this truth if you are to help him or her overcome what has been described as "the acceptable sin of the saints."

Key Scripture

"Be anxious for nothing, but in everything by prayer and supplication, with thanksgiving, let your requests be made known to God; and the peace of God, which surpasses all understanding, will guard your hearts and minds through Christ Jesus" (Phil. 4:6,7).

The truth of this passage comes through clearly in The Living Bible paraphrase which says, "Don't worry about anything; instead, pray about everything. . . ."

Some individuals because of their nature and emotional makeup are more prone to worry than others are, yet anxiety or worry is not justifiable merely because it "comes naturally."

When a friend struggling with this problem asks you, "What do you think I should do about it?" you need to work through several issues. What is the actual cause of concern or worry? What has been done to determine whether or not the issue is valid? For example, if the woman in your Bible study who asks you to pray about "her cancer" has never gone to the doctor for an examination, the first step is to convince her that she needs proper medical diagnosis.

Elderly people usually are quite certain they will run out of money before they die (no matter how much money they have). Getting that person to consult a financial planner or a bank who can help with investments may allay that concern. The person who is worried about personal finances may eliminate that concern by having a budget and learning to stay within it.

Your part as a counselor-friend may be providing emotional support to insure that action is taken. You can also suggest that your friend read *Worry-Free Living* by Dr. Frank Minirth, Dr. Paul Meier, and Don Hawkins.

Has the person who is worried made the matter a definite, concerned issue for prayer? Committing yourself to the keeping of a sovereign God, believing that He is in control of your life, eliminates worry. You can then turn out the light and say, "God, you take the night shift; no need for both of us to be awake. I'm going to sleep!" It works.

Emotional Depression

In phase one of the counseling process you are striving to understand what the problem really is and what is causing it. When your friend comes to you depressed, your first task is to help him or her evaluate the cause of depression.

Insights

Among the causes of depression, look for the following:

- Suppressed anger,
- The feeling of a hopeless situation, or
- Secret habits or problems which result in depression, or
- Physical problems requiring the care of a doctor.

One of the most common causes of depression is the feeling that a person is in a hopeless situation from which there is no escape. For example, a wife with several children and no professional skills, is married to a man who walks out and leaves her with no support. Having no family close by, and little possibility of employment, discouragement turns to despair and eventually to depression.

As you talk with a friend, you begin to determine whether depression is the result of a specific cause (say, when an aerospace engineer, age 47, is laid off because of cutbacks, is overly qualified for menial positions, and can't seem to get back on with a major company), or you are confronted with an individual who seems to suffer from chronic depression without apparent cause. Some of the symptoms of depression are lethargy, indifference to responsibilities, neglected appearance, and emotional flatness.

In situations involving chronic fatigue, I always recommend that the friend go for a complete physical with care given to blood sugar and blood composition. If there is still no apparent physical reason for depression, your friend needs the help of a professional. There is help for the chronically depressed. At times a change of diet or the inclusion of a program of physical exercise in a routine under a physician's supervision or even a low dose of medication (such as lithium), to stabilize a chemical imbalance in the body, relieves depression.

While depression itself is not hereditary, the predisposition to certain personality types which are more susceptible to depression or discouragement can be inherited. Telling a depressed individual to "snap out of it" because God doesn't want the person depressed only drives him deeper into depression. Saying that God cares, and that He will never leave or forsake His child (see Key Scriptures), and understanding that a person has been forgiven and is the child of God, helps an individual to break through depression.

Diagnose the problem but minister to the whole person including the physical, the emotional, and the spiritual.

The Physical Body and Depression

When people tell me about depression, I always ask, "What kind of physical exercise do you get?" and invariably the person gets none or walks around the block thinking "That's exercise!" As the result of counseling people, I have become convinced that physical exertion is one of the best antidotes to depression available today. If I have any question as to a person's physical condition, I send them to a doctor for his counsel as to what they can handle, and then I recommend that the person start walking (build up to a brisk walk of three to five miles at least three times weekly) or get exercise which will increase the heartbeat and the rate of respiration.

Depression and Your Spiritual Life

In striving to isolate the reason for depression, you may discover that an individual is living with something which he or she knows is wrong. Gordon Mac-Donald refers to these people as "secret carriers," individuals who may be struggling with a sin such as an immoral relationship, an addiction to pornography, or a financial shenanigan which he or she knows is wrong. Bringing that problem to light, dealing with it through repentance, confession, and restitution (when necessary) will eliminate depression.

The depressed individual almost always feels that God is distant and that prayer doesn't work. Even John the Baptist, languishing in dark Machaerus Prison probably succumbed to doubt and eventual depression, wondering whether or not Jesus was really the Christ. Depressed individuals usually doubt truths which they really know are valid. In their hearts they know that God has not singled them out as victims of attack, yet they feel isolated and lonely.

When a friend of mine had a heart attack, he lay in the hospital thinking of the speaking engagements he would have to cancel, the writing deadlines that would not be met, and how his meager finances would be stretched by the illness. As he cried out, "Why me, Lord?" he seemed to hear the echo return, "Why not you?" Isaiah 43 reminds us that we will face the valley, the fire, and the flood, but the promise which we must take by faith is that He walks with us.

Key Scriptures
Matthew 28:20, "Lo, I am with you always, even to the end of the age." Also Hebrews 13:5,6, "'I will never leave you nor forsake you.' So we may boldly say: 'The Lord is my helper; I will not fear. What can man do to me?'"

Depression and Your Emotional Life

Recognizing that the spiritual cannot be separated from the emotional, it is necessary to point out that the individual who is depressed not only doubts spiritual truths, but he or she likewise finds it difficult to accept other valid realities ("My wife really doesn't love me, or else she would understand how I feel!"). Here you can help your friend to understand that love is a commitment, and that the husband or wife is standing by the commitment which was made long ago.

An individual's emotions are controlled by the will, and the decision to hold on to reality goes a long way toward breaking through depression (see *Happiness Is a Choice* by Dr. Frank Minirth and Dr. Paul Meier[2]).

In our Guidelines publication "Depression Stoppers"[3] (which is available without cost to those who send a self-addressed, stamped envelope to our office) I point out that praise is a matter of the will. It is one of the tools God has given us to fight the emotional "blahs" of depression. Your friend needs to focus on the goodness of God, His character and faithfulness, and begin to recount the various ways God still smiles upon him or her. The person needs to say, "Lord, I know You are sovereign and in control of the universe. I also believe that You are greater than my depression, and I thank You for what you have done for me and for what you are going to do." Then depression will begin to lift. Happiness *is* a choice!

9

Using the Bible to Counsel Addictive Behavior

As we approach the subject of addictive behavior, you may be tempted to throw up your hands and say, "Whoa, this is too much for me. Someone who is addicted to something needs a professional!" In some cases you are right, and I'll give you guidelines to help you know when to insist that someone get professional help.

In some cases people don't have money for treatment. They don't understand that many professional groups, including the majority of Christian counseling services, have sliding scales to make it possible for almost anyone needing help to receive it.

But often they are not willing to place themselves under the care of a professional whom they do not know or trust. They will, however, turn to you and ask for your help. In some cases it will be the parents or the mate of someone who is hurting who asks, "What do you think I should do?"

Addictive behavior is a pattern of activity which has been established by a person who is emotionally or physically dependent on something or someone. It may be a physical dependency as in substance abuse (alcohol and drugs). In other cases the addictive behavior is an emotional dependency or attachment.

Please understand that my treatment of each subject in this chapter is rather superficial. My goal is to help you identify the addictive problem, and to help your friend see the implication of what he or she is doing to himself and others, as well as the implications of ignoring the issue. In addition, you will learn how to use your Bible to help release the power of the Holy Spirit in the lives of these individuals, for He is the greatest force in all the world when it comes to changing behavioral patterns.

Defining Your Limitations As a Counselor-Friend

When you encounter addictive behavior, you are always confronted with the question, "Can I help?" Much of that answer depends on whether or not the person who is hurting will allow you to help.

These questions provide guidelines in knowing whether to undertake the task of helping or to make a referral and see that the person follows through.

Will the Individual Respond to Confrontation?

If the person with the problem is the one who has come to you and asked, "What do you think I should do?" the confrontation issue is not difficult. It's more complex, however, when a mother says, "I was cleaning my son's room this morning and I found an envelope of white powder I think is cocaine. My son says it isn't his. He says it belonged to the boy who spent the night over the weekend. But I don't believe him. My husband and I think he's a user."

Although we try to avoid it, confrontation is absolutely necessary if a person is to find help. Described as "tough love," this kind of confrontation means that a family is willing to say, "Look, you've got a problem. You know it and we do too, but we love you so much that we insist you get help. We're going to stand with you, but this cannot go on. You have to get help." When you as a coffee cup counselor help another person, the issues of wrongdoing and poor choices must be confronted.

Is the Person Willing to Face the Consequences of His Actions?

In phase two of the counseling process, you are striving to help your friend see the options which are available and the ultimate consequences of his choices. As long as a person refuses to acknowledge he has a problem, he hasn't faced the consequences of his actions. He has to acknowledge that substance abuse or continued addictive behavior will ultimately damage or destroy relationships in his family; the abuse may even take his life.

Does the Person Have the Desire to Change?

Most individuals who come to you for help struggling with some kind of addictive behavior really want help. One of the beautiful things about counseling in the power of the Spirit is that God will help an individual who acknowledges his need and turns to the Lord for help. You are like a midwife whose efforts will be accompanied by pain and travail. When a person comes primarily because someone else wants him to come, to get the "monkey off his back," there is little that you can do. When I see red flags in this regard, I may even tell someone, "Look, I don't think you are ready for us to work together in this problem. I want you to know that I care and I'm available, and when you are ready to work with me, I'm ready to help."

Will the Person Be Completely Honest with Me?

My experience has been that my ability to help someone is directly related to that person's honesty. Deception and dishonesty are marks of individuals who haven't reached the point of being willing to accept help. When people lie to me, I tell them that I can't help them when they are dishonest. I'll still be their friend, but there is no point in either of us wasting time in that kind of situation.

Is the Individual Willing to Be Accountable?

Accountability means a person is willing to show up punctually for appointments and to accept responsibility for his actions. When a person comes to you and wants help, and he also goes to one or two other friends for help, you need to ask the person to make a commitment to one of you. What the other friend wants to do may be exactly what you want, but the way he strives to reach his goal may be at cross purposes with what you are trying to accomplish.

Is the Person Willing to Work with Me?

Is the individual sincere in his willingness to follow the counsel and direction given? As I've already mentioned in this book, when a person is close to you or your family and you think accountability means acknowledging some embarrassing or distasteful things, you may want to refer your hurting friend to someone else for help.

You probably won't get an unqualified and enthusiastic "Yes!" answer to all of these six questions. And as the counseling process flows, there will be times when you may think that you are making little headway, but as long as you see a person is trying to work with you, you can be successful as a coffee cup counselor.

But What if My Friend Doesn't Take My Advice?

There is always the chance that the person you are trying to counsel will ignore your advice and make a choice that you believe is a poor one. What happens to your friendship then?

Your friend will probably avoid you, at least until you let her know that no matter what she does, you will still love her and be her friend. Jesus had that kind of love for His disciples. The week prior to His death at Calvary, He instructed the disciples to love each other as He loved them (see John 13:34-35).

Jesus' love separated acceptance from behavior. At times He reached out to people in love and concern, and they responded by loving Him in return. At other times they turned and walked away, rejecting His love. But His love for them was not diminished by their rejection or personal failure.

You do have limitations as a human counselor; you cannot make people follow your advice, no matter how right you may be. But you can continue to love your friend the way Jesus loved those He ministered to.

Alcohol Abuse

Insights

While the Bible does not teach abstinence when it comes to the use of alcoholic beverages, it does teach moderation. Paul instructed Timothy, "No longer drink only water, but use a little wine for your stomach's sake and your frequent infirmities" (1 Tim. 5:23). The wine of the first century was a beverage with approximately one-third of the alcoholic content of wine today. It also was used as an antiseptic and a medicine. In the story of the good Samaritan (see Luke 10:30–37), the Samaritan poured oil and wine into the wounds of the injured man.

Drunkenness or alcoholic dependency is clearly forbidden by Scripture. Romans 13:13 says, "Let us walk properly, as in the day, not in revelry and drunkenness. . . ." Drunkenness is also singled out as one of the manifestations of the flesh in Galatians 5:21.

Key Scriptures

Ephesians 5:18 instructs: "Do not be drunk with wine, in which is dissipation; but be filled with the Spirit," and Romans 14:21 says, "It is good neither to eat meat nor drink wine nor do anything by which your brother stumbles or is offended or is made weak."

Most of the people who struggle with alcoholism are generally aware that the Bible condemns their problem; they just don't know what to do about it.

Until an individual accepts the fact he or she has a problem with alcohol, you won't be effective as a counselor-helper. At Alcoholics Anonymous individuals begin their testimony with the words, "I am an alcoholic." Recognizing the problem opens the door for solutions. Often your contribution may be to support the alcoholic as he or she begins treatment in a dependency center or in Alcoholics Anonymous.

Motivation in overcoming any dependency has to be stronger than the force of the problem. For a child of God, an understanding that his or her body is the temple of the Holy Spirit of God (see Rom. 12:1,2 and 1 Cor. 6:19) can be a great motive for change. As you work with your friend, try to remember that the Holy Spirit is the agent of behavioral change, and that the individual is responsible and can change. As you pray with and for your friend, expect change, and don't be satisfied until change takes place.

Though some individuals are delivered instantaneously from a dependency on alcohol, most individuals need a great deal of support and help over a period of time. Support from the family and your support as a counselor-friend are vital. When you don't have the time or the emotional energy to offer this support, it is wise to make a referral to an alcohol abuse support group such as Overcomers Outreach, a church-related group. The number of these programs is growing rapidly.

Drug Abuse

Insights

In our generation drug abuse has escalated in an unprecedented fashion, making it the number one problem confronting people today. There is no one set of circumstances which accounts for the use of drugs today. Probably the greatest factor in drug abuse is peer pressure. Among young adults cocaine and crack (freebased cocaine, sold in ready-to-smoke form) have become the drugs of choice. (See Ross Campbell, *Your Child and Drugs,* published by Scripture Press.)

Your job as a counselor-friend includes the determination as to whether your friend has been involved in recreational drug abuse (an occasional user) or has developed an actual drug dependency. An individual who is addicted will stop at nothing to support the craving that his or her body has for drugs, which only underlines the severity of the problem. Drug dependency goes far beyond cocaine. A growing number of individuals, including a large number of women, are dependent on amphetamines and weight control medication. Whether it is cocaine or caffeine (from tea, coffee, or carbonated beverages), a person is addicted when he or she feels physical discomfort ("I get a headache without my coffee") because of its absence.

Scores of individuals who dabble in drugs could have been saved tremendous heartache if someone—like a coffee cup counselor—had picked up on their problem early enough and cared enough to confront the person who was experimenting. When an individual has become addicted and he is physically affected, you will have to refer him to a doctor or drug rehabilitation program where there is supervised help on a 24-hour basis.

Key Scriptures
First Corinthians 6:19,20, "Do you not know that your body is the temple of the Holy Spirit who is in you, whom you have from God, and you are not your own? For you were bought at a price; therefore glorify God in your body and in your spirit, which are God's."

Five powerful words are motives for change: "You are not your own." Then to whom do you belong? To Jesus Christ.

Peter also reminds us of the price of redemption, "Knowing that you were not redeemed with corruptible things, like silver or gold . . . but with the precious blood of Christ" (1 Pet. 1:18,19).

Many people struggling with addictions can successfully be helped by counselor-friends who care enough to ride out the storm. Several suggestions may be helpful as you work through the counseling process.

Remember, from a Christian's perspective, dependence on drugs is a matter of choice. The individual became addicted as the result of choices he or she made. (You are unlikely to counsel with an individual who became addicted to a substance because someone forced drugs on that person.) Likewise, freedom from addiction can come through the decision to resist and live a drug-free life. If drug addiction is harmful (and it is), then it is also sin before God and should be dealt with on that basis.

Complete and absolute dependence upon the Lord is necessary for deliverance. The person who kicks a drug habit "cold turkey" without help is a rare and strong individual; most need help, and that's where you come into the picture as a counselor-friend.

Help your friend develop independence from his peer group. This is probably one of your most important functions. Slogans such as "Just say no!" are well and good, but when an individual's best friends urge him or her to say "Yes!" slogans are meaningless.

Help restructure the environment by offering the support necessary to change the peer group. Being involved in a church or support group where people say, "Man, I can relate to your problem. That's where I was two years ago, but God gave me deliverance and now I'm clean," reverses the process from participation to restraint.

Utilize the power of prayer as you work with a person (more about this in the chapter to follow).

Sexual Addiction

Webster's New Collegiate Dictionary defines the verb "addict" as "to devote or surrender [oneself] to something habitually or obsessively."[1] In relationship to sex this includes obsessive sexual relations, infidelity, and promiscuity.

Obsessive Sexual Relations.

In the context of this book I am not talking about the person who wants to have frequent sexual relations in marriage, or the manner in which he or she finds sexual fulfillment with his mate. Neither am I talking about the youngster who has a perfectly normal curiosity about the sexual functions of his body. I am describing the individual whose sexual appetites have become inflamed to the point of being obsessed with sex just the same as the individual who is addicted to cocaine.

Is such a discussion really necessary in a book like this? If I had written this book even a decade ago, I would probably have answered, "No!" and eliminated this section; however, in the context of our environment and life today, it is necessary.

We are living in a sex-addicted culture, so stated

Pitirim Sorokin, a Harvard University sociologist who made those charges in the early 1970s. Since then, our culture has become so permeated with sex that it oozes from the pores of our national life. Sexually explicit material which would never be allowed in Communist countries, or even in the United States a few decades ago, is now commonplace on American television and in the theater.

In our day the videocassette recorder has moved the X-rated movie from the theater to the home. With today's rating standards, R-rated movies are extremely explicit sexually. In this environment, millions of people who a few years ago would have strongly objected to the sex-saturation of our culture have gradually tolerated it and even embraced it.

Insights

Constant exposure to sex does one of two things: it creates a blasé indifference, or an obsession to the degree that one's perspective becomes totally distorted. Sexual addiction is a perversion of a normal appetite whose fulfillment in marriage has the blessing of God; it becomes a jaded, unsatisfied craving which is wrong. What normally would have satisfied is no longer sufficient. Sexual appetites remain unfulfilled.

How does this happen? In some cases an individual is looking for a missing part of his life: an authentic, valid relationship with someone. Looking for intimacy and companionship, the person goes from one relationship to another, driven by a desire which confuses sex with love. The person suffering from sexual obsession may be the woman who was never held and loved by her father (or her husband) and thus confuses sexual expression with loving relationships. Often it is the male who in his youth did not relate well to women, or to healthy male role-models, and finds a perverse satisfaction in pornography which doesn't talk back or challenge his masculine ego. Having become addicted to pornography, he gradually turns to unsatisfying, unfulfilling sexual encounters.

Key Scriptures

First Corinthians 3:16,17, "Do you not know that you are the temple of God and that the Spirit of God dwells in you? If anyone defiles the temple of God, God will destroy him. For the temple of God is holy, which temple you are." Second Peter 1:3,4, "His divine power has given to us . . . great and precious promises, that through these you may be partakers of the divine nature, having escaped the corruption that is in the world through lust."

How do you help a person overcome this obsession?

Begin by finding out what's being fed into the mind of the person with this problem. Ask the person you are helping to tell you the names and ratings of the last five movies he has seen. Ask how long pornography has played a prominent part in his or her sexual life.

Help a person to see that sexual expression is no substitute for meaningful relationships (more about this in the section under promiscuity).

In helping your friend see himself as God sees him, you will have to label this problem sin and deal with it on that basis. Scripture says, "He who covers his sins will not prosper, but whoever confesses and forsakes them will have mercy" (Prov. 28:13).

Replace negative sexual input with the powerful cleansing of the Word. In 2 Peter 1:4 (quoted above), Peter talks about escaping the corruption and lust of the world through the great promises of God's Word. Long ago the psalmist asked the question, "How can a young man cleanse his way?" and answered, "By taking heed according to Your Word" (Ps. 119:9). Quoting and memorizing Scripture reprograms many of the sensual and lustful images which have affected a person's mind and thinking.

Insist on accountability as you work with your friend over a period of time. This includes honesty, openness and willingness to change.

Promiscuity.

For every married couple today, there is one single adult. Many of them fall into the ranks of the formerly married, individuals who at one time carried on normal sexual relations with a long-term partner but because of death or divorce find themselves single again. For the formerly married, sex was a very ordinary part of their relationship. It represented intimacy, the expression of love, and the emotional and physical release which accompanies orgasm.

For the formerly married, being sexually pure is often not without a struggle. Loneliness and isolation often create situations which cause a person to set aside biblical values for the warmth of another human body. Casual sex has become relatively common for singles who nonetheless consider themselves to be "born again."

In her book *Being a Woman*, Dr. Toni Grant, a popular talk-show psychologist, says:

Many contemporary women with whom I speak have lots of ideas about sexuality and relationships but no standards by which they live and share their bodies. I am constantly getting calls from women who don't know how to say no, who don't even have the language for setting standards of any sort, who are desperately afraid that if they do say no, they will lose the men in their lives.[2]

Casual sex is sex without commitment, and apart from marriage there is no lasting commitment. Today scores of men and women seeking satisfaction confuse sexual experience and commitment. In relationships outside of the commitment of marriage, the woman is the greater loser. To her, sex without marriage is not merely a physical response but an emotional commitment which may not be reciprocated. As Dr. Grant put it, "Any way you slice it, the woman in an uncommitted sexual relationship is between a rock and a hard place. . . . Uncommitted sex has not worked very well for women."[3]

Insights
What God expects of singles, He expects of married couples—sexual purity, which means abstinence before marriage and commitment to one individual, your mate, in marriage. While casual sex may be the norm and even have a measure of acceptance in our culture, it is wrong in the sight of God.

Key Scriptures
First Thessalonians 4:3-5: "For this is the will of God . . . that you should abstain from sexual immorality; that each of you should know how to possess his own vessel [his body] in sanctification and

honor, not in passion of lust, like the Gentiles who do not know God." In this matter, there is no ambiguity and no hedging.

Writing to Timothy, Paul instructed the widowed young women to marry again and assume the responsibilities of a wife and mother, thereby avoiding sexual temptation (see 1 Tim. 5:11–16). Another passage which gives a powerful motive for sexual purity is Romans 12:1,2. In this Paul admonished believers to present their bodies as "a living sacrifice, holy, acceptable to God, which is your reasonable service. And do not be conformed to this world, but be transformed by the renewing of your mind, that you may prove what is that good and acceptable and perfect will of God." Phillips paraphrases the words "do not be conformed to this world" as "Don't let the world force you into its mold."

Of course, promiscuity is not solely the struggle of the formerly married. Sexual temptations confront the teenager and the young adult eager for acceptance. Recent studies indicate that at least 60 percent of teenage girls participate in their first experience because of peer pressure.

The sexually promiscuous person, going from partner to partner, is an insecure individual desperately seeking love and acceptance among partners whose commitment lasts only for a night. Such an individual has emotional needs which can be met only in the context of marriage.

Infidelity in Marriage.

Insights
Unfaithfulness in marriage usually ends in divorce, but it doesn't have to. Although mentioned in Scripture

as valid grounds for divorce (see Matt. 5:31,32; 19:4–9), unfaithfulness can be forgiven. Restoration and healing can take place. That's your goal as a counselor-friend.

When a Christian marriage is affected by an affair, both husband and wife feel guilty. The offending party feels guilty, realizing he or she has sinned before God and broken the promise made at the marriage altar. The offended party also has a sense of guilt because she (or he) thinks, "If only I had met his (or her) needs, if only I had kept myself as beautiful as the other woman (as handsome as the other man), my husband (wife) would not have strayed!"

In dealing with the issue, try to determine if the offended party contributed to the failure of a mate by not meeting the needs of the one who strayed. This does not remove the responsibility from the unfaithful spouse but helps the offended partner accept responsibility for his or her part in the marriage breakdown.

At times, though, the failure of one person to meet the needs of the other is not the issue at all. Ask a group of people, "How many does it take for a marriage to fail?" and the majority of people will respond, "Two!" But the fact is that when only one person in a marriage says, "I don't want to be married to you any more; I want my freedom," a marriage is finished.

A husband or wife may deeply love his or her mate, but when confronted with sexual opportunity the individual gives in to temptation. Afterward the person deeply regrets what took place. This situation offers the greatest opportunity for forgiveness and healing.

In Chapter 7 we dealt with the issue of forgiveness. This never comes easy, especially when the deepest of all relationships is violated, but healing can take place. Just as a broken bone can heal stronger than before the accident took place, a restored marriage can make a relationship deeper and more treasured because of the crisis which has been weathered.

Homosexuality

Insights

The traditional Judeo-Christian position is that homosexuality, among other practices, is condemned by God. Paul included this lifestyle in cataloguing the former failures of the Corinthians in 1 Corinthians 6:10 and 11.

Key Scriptures

The Old Testament clearly condemned the practice. Leviticus 18:22 says, "You shall not lie with a male as with a woman. It is an abomination." (Also see Lev. 20:13.) The New Testament continues the prohibition. First Corinthians 6:11, "And such were some of you. But you were washed, but you were sanctified, but you were justified in the name of the Lord Jesus and by the Spirit of our God." In Romans 1 Paul spoke of those who received the revelation of God and rejected it.

> For this reason God gave them up to vile passions. For even their women exchanged the natural use for what is against nature. Likewise also the men, leaving the natural use of the woman, burned in their lust for one another, men with men committing what is shameful, and receiving in themselves the penalty of their error which was due (Rom. 1:26,27).

In counseling with individuals who have practiced homosexuality, the important thing to remember is that sexual preference is a choice which we make as an act of the will, not a genetic predilection which a person cannot control. At this writing there is absolutely no scientific evidence or support for the gay position that an individual has been "trapped" by his genetic code which would relieve him or her of his responsibility in the sight of God.

For God to condemn an individual for a practice which he or she could not help would be unjust. The fact is that homosexuality is one of many practices which can be forgiven by God, and with His forgiveness comes His enabling power to change—something which the church is often strangely silent in proclaiming.

Be cautious in labeling individuals. One or two encounters of a homosexual nature no more make an individual a homosexual than one or two drinks make an individual an alcoholic. Consistent homosexual practice, however, does result in that person being a homosexual.

My experience has been that individuals who come for counseling with this problem fall into two categories: those who want *acceptance* in this lifestyle and those who realize their lives are displeasing to God and want to change. For this second group there is every reason to believe that the Holy Spirit will bring deliverance. While it is difficult to reorient sexual preferences, it is not impossible any more than it is for an individual who has been delivered from alcoholism to resist when he encounters alcohol.

In counseling with homosexuals, remember that God loves the individual. It is the sin which God condemns. All too often we condemn the person along with his sin. Strive to let your friend know that you love and accept him or her as a human being.

Compulsive Eating Disorders

Our English word *bulimia* is a transliteration of the Greek word which means "great hunger." It is an eating disorder involving gorging on food, followed by self-induced vomiting or purging. Its opposite is anorexia, self-induced starvation. Both are serious disorders. The possibility of your helping as a coffee cup counselor is dependent on your following the guidelines which begin this chapter. As with other addictions your greatest contribution may be to help your friend recognize the seriousness of the problem and then guide and support the individual in receiving professional help.

Insights

When emotional needs are met we act in a responsible manner, but when needs are not met a spectrum of irresponsible activities follow, which may include eating disorders. One of the most difficult things for someone struggling with this issue is to admit there is a problem. Usually these individuals try to hide the problem, not wanting family or friends to know what is happening.

Take, for example, Dori, who wrote the following to me when she discovered that her roommate, Pat, was bulimic:

> Right now I am just sick to my stomach, I am so upset. The problem is Pat [my roommate]. I guess I had no idea how messed up that girl is until the last few weeks. I have noticed that she always disappears after meals but I thought it was only to get out of the dishes. She has been doing this for a long time because [her last year's roommate] discovered it when she was living with her.

I am crushed. I deplore what Pat is inside and yet I am so sad and broken-hearted for her, I can't even explain it. The thing that I feel the very worst about is that I have lost all respect for her as a person; she is disgusting, or rather what she is doing is disgusting.

Dori told me later that Pat's dad wanted a boy when she was born and always felt that "Patricia" should have been "Patrick." As she grew up her dad never expressed as much affection for her as he did with the other children. Money? He had plenty of it and saw that she attended the best boarding schools and had nice clothes and a sports car. "I know her problem was really the result of her relationship with her dad," Dori said in recounting the year she lived with Pat.

Dori was able to separate her feelings for the girl from her revulsion for her problem and remained her friend. On the other hand, Pat never admitted the problem and continued with the pattern into her adult life.

Key Scriptures
Romans 12:1,2 reminds us that our bodies are to be "a living sacrifice holy, acceptable to God." First Corinthians 3:16,17 says our bodies are temples of the Holy Spirit and that the Spirit of God literally indwells our bodies, giving us a motive for health.

Eating disorders can be serious addictive problems, equally as dangerous as drug and alcohol addiction, and cannot be treated lightly. While you may feel the problem is more serious than you can handle, you may be the link between disaster and life through your friendship, warmth, compassion, and care. You do make a difference.

Now, let's go on to our final chapter as I share some more guidelines which make for success in coffee cup counseling.

10

Success in Coffee Cup Counseling

What is success in counseling? For me, it is helping a person find the will of God for his life, providing the support which is necessary for that person to move toward God's will, and then seeing the individual grow in his relationship with Christ. In the process, something of my life, my emotions, my intellect, my time, and my energies are invested in that person.

I have a set of gold cuff links with a monogram on one link and a watch on the other. I suppose that I have worn them no more than a dozen times in my life. I would hate to lose them—not because of their value, which is incidental—but because they were a gift, a token of a victory which God wrought in the life of a man who had maintained a homosexual lifestyle for most of his adult life.

Listening to my radio program in San Francisco, he concluded that I could help him, called for an appointment, and began flying more than four hundred miles each way once a week for counseling. Through the same counseling process I have used in this book, that man came to a saving knowledge of Jesus Christ and eventually learned that God had a different plan for his life. The break with his former lifestyle was not an easy one.

Habits and practices which have been years in the making are not eliminated in a matter of a few weeks. But they can be broken. And he ultimately found God's grace to reorient his lifestyle and habits. Writing to the Corinthians, Paul mentions homosexuality and then says, speaking of those who were now in the church, "And such were some of you. But you were washed, but you were sanctified, but you were justified in the name of the Lord Jesus and by the Spirit of our God" (1 Cor. 6:11).

Success in coffee cup counseling is seeing individuals whose lives were headed in the wrong direction make changes which give them a hope and a new future.

It is watching children grow up in a home which would have been destroyed had not God used you in some way to help a friend realize how foolish it would have been to throw away a marriage for the thrill of a make-believe, illicit relationship.

It is watching individuals who could not function without the support of a vast rainbow of drugs stabilize their emotions, begin to grow emotionally and spiritually, and relate to life in a way they never have before.

Success in counseling is helping individuals rise to their full, God-given potential, not because you are so bright or clever, but because you learned the importance of letting the Holy Spirit chip away at the rough edges of the person with whom you worked, allowing Christ to live in the life of your friend.

Yes, I freely admit that I don't win every round. There are times when I walk away from a situation feeling that I have failed, thinking to myself, "Did I miss something? Was there anything else I should have done to make a difference?" Some things we must learn by experience, and every person who becomes proficient in coffee cup counseling will have learned from his or her mistakes.

As I look back over three decades of counseling and training others to help people, I recognize that success in counseling is the interaction of God's Holy Spirit in the life of a person using me as a catalyst and channel. I also believe that there are some things you can do to turn your friend's failure into success.

Success in Counseling Comes by Persevering Until a Relationship Has Stabilized

When my son, Steve, was in the final year of his college program, he spent a summer in Northern Luzon in the Philippines working among a tribal group. His area of training was in biomedical engineering, and he wanted some "hands-on" medical experience in cooperation with a medical team.

Apart from not being able to communicate freely with the people because he didn't know the language, his greatest frustration was to see someone who was very ill, give him penicillin or medication which would cure the problem, see the person start taking the medicine but quit because he was feeling better, and then sustain a far more serious attack than the first, simply because he didn't finish the round of antibiotics.

Breaking off counseling too soon does the same thing. The process of restoration may take time. No progress takes place in a straight line. People will make improvement, fail, try again, and fail again. Only when they stop trying do they quickly begin to slide downhill in the counseling process.

How do you handle failures? In just the same way you help a child learning to walk—you help pick up your friend, get him walking again, and gradually turn loose. In helping a friend gain strength and maturity to overcome persistent failures, I take the person through this process:

WHAT HAPPENED?

WHAT WAS YOUR RESPONSE?

WHAT SHOULD HAVE BEEN YOUR RESPONSE?

HOW CAN YOU RECTIFY THE PROBLEM?

Some marriages should never have taken place. Bob and Beverly often thought theirs was one of them. She got pregnant when they were still in their teens, and under pressure from parents they married. Bob worked as a laborer in construction, and his weekend "hobby" was vegetating in front of the TV with a six-pack of beer and a bag of potato chips.

Beverly was bright and energetic. As the years went by, apart from their children, they had less and less in common. Eventually, Beverly met a friend who was challenging and caring, and the friendship deepened into a lesbian relationship. Beverly moved out with her children, and for two years lived with her friend. Then, she went for counseling and found Jesus as her Savior.

Determined to do what God wanted, she broke off the relationship with the friend, and came home—

something her husband also wanted. But being together again didn't change their personalities or the big differences in their ability to think. Arguments were bound to happen and they did, frequently. As Beverly told me about one, we worked through the process (as outlined above).

"What happened?" I asked, and she told me.

"What was your response?"

"Well, I told him he was a stupid jerk . . ." (and a few other things that weren't any more complimentary).

"O.K. What should have been your response?"

"Well, I suppose I should have cooled off and then tried to tell him how I felt about the issue."

"What do you think you need to do to make the situation right?"

After thinking for a few minutes she answered, "I suppose I need to apologize for my attitude and what I said."

She did.

Re-establishing broken relationships is not a do-it-once-and-you're-finished-with-that-for-life kind of thing. Continuing problems can be worked through with the same questions: What happened? How did you respond? How should you have responded? What do you need to do or say to correct the situation?

Be Empathetic and Warm in Your Relationship with the People You Help

There is a difference between empathy and sympathy! Empathy means "I care." To a degree, you hurt with your friend, but if your emotions carry you away so that you lose control, both of you will need help.

Does this mean that you never express emotions? That is not what I am suggesting. Sometimes relating to your friend on a warm, personal basis is the best therapy you can give.

Dr. William Glasser, author of the book *Reality Therapy,* believes that if just one individual believes in another person, that individual can be the anchor to reality which keeps the person from slipping over the precipice of irrationality. You as a coffee cup counselor may be that anchor!

There have been occasions when I absolutely could not persuade an individual that he was headed for disaster. As the saying goes, a person convinced against his will is of the same opinion still. In those instances, I don't preach, pounding him over the head with my entreaties. I'm simply there, and my presence as a caring, empathetic person allows the friend to get some of the rebellion out of his heart. Having relieved some of that emotion, he may begin to listen to reason.

Jim was like that. Having grown up in a home which adhered to strict discipline and a rather pharisaical approach to what Christians do and don't do (you don't drink, smoke, go to movies, or associate with those who do), Jim married and became quite successful in his profession. He went to church and was active. Then when middle-aged boredom set in, rather foolishly he began to experiment with some of the things he would never have touched a few years before. One thing led to another. Then one day he found himself in a situation where it suddenly hit him, "You have really played the fool." Being ashamed of himself and fearing that his conduct could bring embarrassment to his family, he planned to take his life in such a way that it would appear to be an accident, so the family could collect insurance. But before he did that, he told me what he planned to do.

I didn't need to convince him that what he had done was foolish and that taking his life would only bring tremendous pain to his family; he was already convinced.

I couldn't have out-argued him even if I had wanted; he was far too clever for me.

I didn't have to help him see himself as he was; he saw himself far more clearly than I did.

It wasn't necessary for me to help him discover God's will; he already knew what he needed to do.

All I could do was weep with him and listen . . . and listen. And pray.

Then he had a series of long, heart-to-heart talks with his wife. He discovered that the strong will which made him successful in business intimidated his wife. Every disagreement turned into a battle he had to win, and she became frustrated trying to express her feelings. Eventually she stopped trying and developed a life of her own.

He also began to renew his relationship with the Lord—not on the basis of what he thought others expected of him (especially what he had practiced as a youngster), but what he felt God expected.

His faith became deeper, more intense. He separated the wheat from the chaff and held that which was good. Years have passed, and that struggle has long since faded into the oblivion of God's forgetfulness, and this man has subsequently played a very important part in God's work. But what he learned might have been lost had I pushed too hard in trying to do what only God could accomplish.

Discover the Power of Prayer
in Effecting Change

Earlier in this book, I encouraged you to pray as you counsel, asking the Lord to give you insight and wisdom as you work with your friend. Praying *with* your friend should be just as natural and relaxed as the conversation you have with him or her. Sometimes I pray with a person as we begin a session of coffee cup counseling. I may say something like, "Terry, before we get into this today, let's take a few minutes and ask the Lord to guide us."

On other occasions, I'll pray with a person during the session, or lead him in prayer, saying words of confession which I ask him to make his own. When there is sin which needs to be confessed, I say something like, "Look, you've told me clearly what the problem is. Let's tell the Lord what you've just told me." I'll lead in prayer briefly for a few seconds, and then say, "You put it in your own words and tell the Lord just what you've told me!" Almost always there is a breaking and rending of the emotions as the confession comes out in prayer.

Prayer is a kind of spiritual therapy through which God forgives sin and the Holy Spirit cleanses a person's conscience. It is a means of relieving tension which allows fruitful communication to follow. It is extremely difficult to tell the Lord how you feel about an issue, hold hands with the person with whom you are in conflict, and then hurl angry words at that person.

When I am counseling with a couple who are struggling with problems, I will often ask them to make a commitment to pray with each other for a few minutes each day, grasping hands together and letting the words just flow out of their heart. The next time we are together, I ask how prayer is affecting their relationship and problem.

As a counselor-friend you need to pray for the person you are trying to help, asking God to undertake the healing and restoration of the one who has come to you. When I pray and ask God's help, my expectancy is increased. Having asked Him to do something, I expect problems to be resolved.

The power of prayer in counseling has yet to be fully appreciated and practiced, but it is one of the greatest resources available to us.

Flow with the Spirit

Writing to the Galatians, Paul cataloged the acts of the sinful nature—the problems that bring many people to us—and then contrasted the fruit of the Spirit with these. He wrote, "Those who belong to Christ Jesus have crucified the sinful nature with its passions and desires. Since we live by the Spirit, let us keep in step with the Spirit" (Gal. 5:24,25). The word Paul uses, translated "keep in step," means "march" or "follow." Yes, you can counsel in the Spirit as you pray, utilize the Word of God, and guide your friend into the path of God's will.

This, of course, means that *you* need to be filled with the Spirit, making Christ Lord of your life, allowing His Word to guide you in your personal life.

As David wrote long ago, "The godly man is a good counselor because he is just and fair and knows right from wrong" (Ps. 37:30,31 LB). May God help you to be that person as you help others.

Keep the coffee pot in good working order!

Notes

1 You Can Help People!
    1. William F. Gingerich, *Shorter Lexicon of the Greek New Testament* (Chicago: The University of Chicago Press, 1965), 162.
    2. "Psychiatry on the Couch," *Time,* April 2, 1979, 74.
    3. "Psychoanalysis: Identity Crisis," The Washington Post, *Insight* section, and "Psychiatry on the Couch," Ibid.
    4. Karl Menninger, *Whatever Became of Sin?* (New York: Bantam Books, 1978), 34.

2 Getting Started
    1. Jay Adams, *Competent to Counsel* (Grand Rapids: Baker Book House, 1970) 76.

4 The Counseling Process
    1. Frank Pittman, *Private Lies*: *Infidelity and the Betrayal of Intimacy* (New York: W. W. Norton and Company) in "Secrets of Staying Together," *Reader's Digest*, March, 1989, 152.
    2. William Glasser, *Reality Therapy* (New York, NY: Harper and Row, Publishers, 1975), xi-xxix.
    3. Frank Pittman, *Private Lies*, 151.

5 Diagnose the Problem but Treat the Whole Person
    1. Lawrence Crabb, Jr., "Moving The Couch Into the Church," *Christianity Today,* September 22, 1978, 17, 18.

2. Ibid.
3. Ibid.

6 Counseling "by the book" or by the Book?
1. Bernie Zilbergeld, "A Psychotherapist Looks at What's Wrong with His Profession," *The Register,* August 7, 1986, Section J.I.
2. David Holzman, *(The Washington Post),* December 6, 1986, *Insight* section, 17.
3. H. Newton Malony, "Is Neurosis for Real?" *Christianity Today,* March 20, 1987, 68.
4. John 14:16,26; 15:26; 16:7.
5. Rom. 15:16; 1 Cor. 6:11; 2 Thess. 2:13.
6. Adams, *Competent,* 25.
7. William Kirk Kilpatrick, *Psychological Seduction* (Nashville: Thomas Nelson, 1983), 10.
8. H. Newton Malony, *Neurosis,* 67.

7 Using the Bible in Counseling Relational Problems
1. Ted Engstrom with Robert Larson, *Integrity* (Waco: Word Books, 1987), 10.
2. See Beverly Caruso, *Loving Confrontation* (Minneapolis: Bethany House, 1988).

8 Using the Bible in Counseling Emotional Problems
1. Gingerich, *Shorter Lexicon,* 96.
2. Frank Minirth and Paul Meier, *Happiness is a Choice* (Grand Rapids, Michigan: Baker Book House, 1988).
3. Harold J. Sala, "Depression Stoppers" (Laguna Niguel, California: Guidelines Press, n.d.).

9 Using the Bible to Counsel Addictive Behavior
1. Henry Bolsey Woolf, ed., *Webster's New Collegiate Dictionary* (Springfield, Massachusetts: Merriam-Webster, Inc., 1979), 13.
2. Toni Grant, *Being a Woman* (New York: Random House, 1988), 51.
3. Ibid., 52.
4. Used by permission from the author.